5thSet for Methodology & Competition

Cory Swede Burns

This work may not be reproduced in any manner without express, written permission from the author.

Copyright 2015 by Cory Swede Burns

The author disclaims any responsibility for consequences resulting from the misapplication of the information in this book.

Consult a doctor before beginning any physical exercise regimen.

Cover artwork by IRON&emotion

Book design by Sin Leung

ISBN 9781973289630

Thank you, to Sin, specifically, for pushing me to write this book.

Thank you, to the Keyhole Barbell powerlifting team: You are my family and I'm very proud of you all.

Thank you, to every lifter who has put their faith in me and in this way of training, continually reaffirming my own faith and proving that 5thSet is a nonpareil methodology.

Use **#TeamSwede** and **#5thSet** when posting training videos and pictures to social media.

www.5thSet.black

A Note from The Author

This work was originally published in the summer of 2015, exclusively as an E-book.

By the close of that year, 5thSet was already one of the top five most used methods of training in the world, according to a survey of over 1000 lifters, conducted by elitefts.com. Its popularity has only continued to grow from there, and at this point I'd be willing to wager 5thSet is the most commonly used method of training in the sport of powerlifting in the United States. There is good reason for that.

The widespread success of lifters using the method was certainly a contributing factor to me being voted 2016 Powerlifting Coach of the Year. To be fair, I did coach quite a few of the best lifters in the world to their best performances to date that same year, but with all of those lifters I used the 5thSet methodology. Whether this is your first time reading this book, or it was a purchase you made for the convenience and warmth of a tangible incarnation of something you already love: I know you will enjoy it.

Please be certain to read the follow-up to this book, 5thSet: Evolutions, available for purchase through www.5thSet.black - as an E-book, and also very soon in paperback, like this one. Our website is also a great resource for 5thSet products and services, including coaching, coaching certifications, seminars, apparel and more.

Introduction 1

Training 3

Beyond the beginning 5

Setting up your 5thSet program 7
   Estimating 1RM's 7
   5thSet Basics 8
   Considering recovery 10
   Selecting a training schedule 11

Running 5thSet 14
   Progressions: 14
   Sample program 17
   Training Log 20
   Peaking for a Meet 23

Meet Day 28
   Sample attempt selection 30
   Bench Press Attempt Selection: 31
   A few more key points of advice I want to touch on regarding meet day: 32

After the Meet (What Now?) 35

Building a Custom 5thSet Program 38
   Mechanically Similar Movement (MSM) 39
   The 2nd pressing day: 42
   5thSet custom program recap: 43

The Competition Lifts 45
   The Squat (mid-bar) 46
   The Bench Press 48
   The Deadlift (Conventional) 51
   The Deadlift (Sumo) 53
   How to warm up 54

Gear check 57
   Footwear 57

    Lifting Belt 57
    Wrist Wraps.. 58
    Knee Sleeves 59
    Knee Wraps 59
    Chalk 61

MSM lists for each lift... 62
    For The Squat (Mid-Bar) 63
    For The Bench Press 64
    For The Deadlift (Conventional) 65

Preferred Assistance Exercises 68
    Chins/Pull ups 68
    Barbell Rows 68
    Barbell Shrugs.. 69
    Chest Supported Dumbbell Rows 70
    Chest Supported Dumbbell Shrugs..................................... 71
    Two Board Press.. 71
    Wide Grip Bench Press 72
    Incline Dumbbell Press 72
    Rolling Tricep Extension 73
    Seated Military Press 74
    Standing Overhead Press 75
    Dips 75
    Side Raise.. 75
    Rear Raise 76
    Cable Tricep Extension 76
    Hammer Curls 76
    Band Pull-Apart 77
    Reverse Hyper Machine... 78
    Pull Through 78
    Leg Curl.. 79
    Calf Raises... 79

The Elephant In The Room 81
    Performance Enhancing Drugs and Powerlifting 81

The takeaway.. 82
Is this a program designed for lifters who take steroids?...... 84
A brief word about PED use in females and how it effects this program.. 86

Frequently Asked Questions..88

The Templates 96
Deadlift- Technique/Speed Template, Assistance Variant #1 97
Deadlift- Technique/Speed Template, Assistance Variant #2 100
Deadlift- Technique/Speed Template, Assistance Variant #3 103
Deadlift- Technique/Speed Template, Assistance Variant #4 106
Low Recoverability- Deadlift- Technique/Speed Template . 121
Low Recoverability- Squat- Technique/Speed Template.... 124
Low Recoverability- Deadlift- Technique/Speed Template . 127
Low Recoverability- Squat- Technique/Speed Template.... 130
Bench Only Template... 133
Garage/Basement Template- Deadlift- Technique/Speed .. 136
Garage/Basement Template- Squat- Technique/Speed..... 139

Introduction

It's all been done before:

You may have heard it said and, for the most part, I will concede that there is nothing new under the sun. The concepts you will find in this program are no exception. The synergy from the combined application of these concepts, however, is something new entirely and is what sets this program apart from everything else. 5thSet is truly greater than the sum of its parts. And that is saying something, because every part is good.

All of my life, in every situation and experience, I have taken the meat and spit out the bone. That is to say, from whatever anyone had to teach me or that I have observed, or tested, or succeeded at, or failed: I took what was useful and later discarded what I found to be unnecessary. 5thSet is a product of that; a unique, easy to use and extremely effective *combination* of ideas (some of which have been used in programs from the start of modern strength training). Everything is systemized; everything is scalable; everything is effective and everything has a purpose.

I used Prilepin's table to determine the target volume. I found a novel way to self-regulate, while keeping almost all of the work at a given percentage. I felt this was important, because in my experience that strategy has yielded a better overall increase than training with a system which has the working sets spread across a large percentage range. I have learned over the years that there is a wide variance in recoverability from person to person, for a number of reasons, and this program addresses that with the 5thSet "fail-out" feature, as well as template variants to suit the individual needs of lifters with lower or higher recovery thresholds. The "fail-out" feature is a kind of fail-safe that can shorten the length of time between the typical deloads when a lifter has accumulated enough fatigue for that to be necessary.

Introduction

Otherwise, every 6th microcycle is a deload. (Relax, I will explain what all of those things are, as well as anything else you might not understand.)

In the ten years or so since I put the first version of this program together, I haven't found anything to be as effective on the long term or as easy to manipulate from a coaching standpoint

Training

"Programs are a hassle. Can't I just train?"

The short answer is yes, if you are actually training. In fact, if you are training, that right there is one of the largest pieces of the puzzle when it comes to succeeding in competitive powerlifting, knocked out of the way already. But I have a feeling you are asking the wrong question. Let me explain.

I have, at different periods in my life, had the misfortune of training at commercial gyms for years at a time. Anyone who has done this for any length of time knows that you get into a schedule and end up coming on the same days and around the same times. This makes it almost impossible to ignore certain things about the other people who show up consistently during those times, if you have any amount of situational awareness.

There are always outliers and exceptions to every rule, but I've noticed that most people who actually lift weights in these places never really get any stronger, or bigger, or leaner. There is no improvement. The same 240-pound guy you see benching 315 for a double with horrible form, will probably be on that same bench in 2 years working with that same technique and that same weight.

On the treadmills and ellipticals? The same row of the same women, 15-20 pounds overweight, sweating their asses off, still looking exactly the same as they did 2 years prior. Everything same, same, same.

This has always blown my mind, because if I was working out consistently for 2 years with no improvement I'd probably quit and buy a bottle of bourbon; rethink my goals. Maybe I would start scrap-booking, or try my hand as a cult leader, but I definitely would not keep doing what I had been doing.

Back to these people, what do they all have in common? Well, for one, they aren't training. Any of them would probably tell you that they train, but to call what they are doing "training" would be a misnomer. It is likely that none of them are or have worked with an experienced coach or they would be employing reasonable technique and following a program of some kind, anyway.

But that guy repping 315 is pretty strong. He must do some training, right?

Not necessarily.

No matter how strong you are, if you are still hitting the same number you were six months ago, you're not really training in my mind, you're maintaining; you're exercising, just like the ladies on the treadmills.

You're existing. It is possible that the ladies have improved their VO2 max in that time, or some other measure of cardiovascular capacity. So, they might actually be doing better than you, but don't worry, I doubt it.

That is just it: training is something that improves your capacity, capability and performance. If those things aren't improving, to at least some degree, I would not call what you're doing training. Sure, you lift weights, jog, do chin ups, exercise or keep active or whatever; but if you aren't making progress, training is what you need to do, not what you are doing. You're confusing yourself by calling it that.

Can't you just train?

Yeah, but in order to actually do that you are probably going to need some kind of systemized approach like a program. Sorry Charlie.

Beyond the beginning

In the beginning, anything works. What I mean to say is that just about any method of training which involves squat, bench press and deadlift will allow you to get stronger at those three lifts, assuming that you are an absolute beginner. Any seasoned vet in the lifting world will probably be happy to wax nostalgic with you, talking about the huge strides they were able to make in their first couple of years of training. I know I don't mind. I'm pretty sure I did my first real program at 15 years old, although I'd been lifting in my basement before that. I got it from Fred Hatfield, Dr. Squat. After about a year of lifting I did my first bench contest at my high school and benched 300 pounds. (That same week I deadlifted 405 for the first time.) Only two years later I benched 405, which was around the time I graduated.

Ahh... progress came so easily back then. It took me only 2 years to add 105 pounds to an already impressive bench for someone my size and age. Pay attention to this part: the next 105 pounds took me about 12 years or so.

Progress in strength is not usually a linear thing and there are myriad reasons for that. This is a tough lesson for a lot of people to learn, I know it was for me. I wanted to train hard for a few weeks and then max on all the lifts and I wanted to lift more every time I maxed.

Unfortunately, in reality, that's not the way things work. It is very difficult for an experienced lifter to improve substantially on all three lifts during the same training cycle. It took me a long time to realize, however, that it is possible.

I always knew, almost instinctively, that doing a lot of high percentage work for both squat and deadlift during the same training cycle was just not the best idea. I look back at programs I wrote 15 years ago reflecting that obvious truth and I still feel

Beyond the beginning

the same way now. The two movements are too similar, mechanically, and you run into overlap/overuse with too much high percentage volume for both.

More times than not, especially with less than masterful lifters, pushing both movements in this manner will end in an overuse injury. (If not multiple injuries.) *"If you chase two rabbits, both get away."* Sound advice for any application and this is a major tenet of the 5thSet program.

But let's rewind for a second, back to the part where I said it *is possible* to improve substantially on all three lifts during the same training cycle. Here is how that is accomplished: *improved technical proficiency.*

You pick one lift and train it for moderate relative volume, with a percentage that is light enough to allow you to make corrections in technique, but heavy enough so that those corrections will have carryover into a max lift. For this lift you are going to try to move the bar as quickly as possible while maintaining excellent technique.

Setting up your 5thSet program

For each training cycle, a maximum of two of the three main lifts will be trained using the 5thSet Protocol. The way those two lifts are selected is by first choosing which, between the squat and deadlift, will be the technique/speed protocol lift for a given training cycle. The remaining two lifts are the 5thSet lifts for that cycle. You may choose to do bench press with the technique/speed protocol, also, but squat and deadlift should never be performed with the 5thSet protocol at the same time.*

Pick, between the squat and deadlift, the one that you feel is your better lift. (Not necessarily the higher number, but the one you feel is more technically proficient.) The other lift will be your technique/speed lift. So, if you think your squat is amazing and flawless and your deadlift, not so much, you will be choosing deadlift as your tech lift for your first training cycle. If you think you are just as good at both, fine. Pick either one. This lift will be performed starting with 70% of your 1RM, for five sets of three reps. Five pounds will be added to the bar every microcycle. When selecting a template, choose one which reflects this decision.

Estimating 1RM's

It is very important that you use current 1RM's to figure out your starting weights. If you have taken a max for a lift within the last few weeks in the gym, that's fine. If not, I want you to take a rep max to estimate for your max. Pick a weight that you are sure you can get for a minimum of three reps. Don't be careless about this, if you are able to get more than ten reps this won't work. So, a weight you can get for a minimum of three *difficult* reps. Warm up to that weight and then perform as many reps as possible.

Setting up your 5thSet program

Find the number of reps you were able to perform in the table on the next page. Multiply the corresponding coefficient number by the number of pounds or kilos you lifted. This will give you your estimated max for any given lift.

Reps Performed	Multiplication Coefficient
1	1
2	1.04
3	1.07
4	1.1
5	1.14
6	1.17
7	1.21
8	1.24
9	1.28
10	1.33
Reps x Coefficient = Est. Max	

5thSet Basics

- You choose one lift for the Technique/Speed protocol- 5 sets of 3 reps, performed with 70% 1RM. Five pounds will be added to this lift per microcycle. **This protocol cannot be used for wrapped squats.**
- Both remaining lifts are set at 80% (77.5% for first mesocycle) and performed on their respective days with the 5thSet protocol- four sets of two reps, followed by an "all-out" **5thSet** of as many reps as possible (AMRAP).
- Five pounds will be added to the 5thSet protocol (80%) lifts for five microcycles, or until the lifter is unable to

Setting up your 5thSet program

perform more than three reps on the 5thSet and "fails-out", whichever comes *first*. At this point a deload microcycle is performed and you start a new training cycle (mesocycle).

- This program is designed for a lifter to train 3 days per week and 4 sessions per 9 day microcycle. (Example: Monday- Session 1, Wednesday- Session 2, Friday- Session 3, Monday-Session 4, Wednesday- Session 1, and so on)

- You select one of the templates based on the protocols you've chosen, as well as your individual weak points; or you build a custom program.

    o Round *down* all percentages to the nearest 5-pound increment. If the percentage lands on an even five-pound increment, start with 5 full pounds *less* than that number.

        - In other words, if your max bench is 300 pounds, and bench is a 5thSet protocol lift, 80% of that number is 240, a five-pound increment. In this case you would round down a full five pounds and start with 235 pounds. If it was your *first training cycle*, 77.5% of 300 is 232.5, which is not an even 5-pound increment. In this case you would round down to the nearest 5-pound increment and start with 230 pounds.

- All three lifts should be filmed, reviewed and corrected every microcycle. This is especially true for novice lifters, but experienced lifters will benefit as well.

If you don't know enough to police your own technique, hire someone who does. Since the advent of the internet, it's pretty

Setting up your 5thSet program

simple to get ahold of and hire some of the best coaches in the world, online, and most of them, including myself, offer technique/video review for a small fee. If you can't afford to hire someone, do your best to emulate the technique of a proficient lifter with a similar style to your own and correct yours to that standard.

Considering recovery

Bear in mind this is not in any way a "get in shape" or "stay in shape" workout program. It's not the program for the aging guy or girl who used to lift and wants to stay active in their golden years. This is a strength based program and though it can be used by anyone trying to get stronger, 5thSet is geared toward people who want to compete in the sport of raw powerlifting. It was designed with the express intent of getting the lifter as strong as possible in spite of any obstacles or hurdles of circumstance. It is easily modified, with those things considered, to be the most rapidly productive possible means of generating gains in strength on the long term. As a result, it can be extremely difficult and taxing at times, both mentally and physically. Be vigilant about getting enough rest and do everything in your power to recover between training sessions.

The 5thSet program is a lot of hard work with relatively high percentages. As I said before, recoverability and adaptability can vary greatly between lifters. If you find yourself struggling to get through your sets after your first few microcycles, hang in there. Your work capacity should improve quickly. This can take longer for some people than others. Most lifters will find that by their second mesocycle with the program they are able to get through the work and finish the five microcycles between deloads more easily. Some lifters, however, have a really hard time adjusting to the volume of work at the prescribed intensity. If this feels like more work than you should be doing and you find that your body

Setting up your 5thSet program

always still feels devastated going *in* to training sessions, consider switching to one of the **Lower Recoverability Templates** after finishing the deload at the end of your first mesocycle. Doing this in some cases can actually improve your rate of progress.

You have the option of either starting with one of the template variations I have provided or customizing a program. If you are newer to lifting or this is your first time following a program like this, you need to stick to one of the templates for a while. It will teach you the framework and help you lay the groundwork you need. Even though this program is easy to organize, in the beginning you need to focus on things like digging into the work in front of you, getting enough sleep, eating enough and just getting more time under the bar in general, not picking exercises and customizing things. I want to reiterate that the templates are a good choice even for very advanced lifters. They have all been tested and proven to work, many times over. Not one of those templates did I just make up for this book, and anything I have tried that didn't work out has been discarded. They have all been used successfully by myself, a wide variety of my clients, or both.

Selecting a training schedule

On this program, you will only be doing three training sessions worth of work during any given week. The fourth session falls on the first training day of the following week. In other words, you will need to pick three days that you want to be your scheduled training days every week. If you feel that you need to be locked in to a seven-day training schedule and you have to hit certain lifts on the same day every week, you can absolutely do that. **Just do it with another program.** 5thSet is not designed to run that way.

Setting up your 5thSet program

Options for scheduled days							
1	Mon		Wed		Fri		
2		Tues		Thurs		Sat	
3	Mon		Wed			Sat	
4		Tues		Thurs			Sun
5	Mon			Thurs		Sat	
6			Wed		Fri		Sun

Above are six choices for schedules that work for 5thSet. Obviously sometimes life shows up and you need to deviate from the plan, but pick one of these and make it the plan. I will explain in greater detail later, that some people will choose to split the longer sessions into two smaller sessions and finish second half on the following day. These schedule options allow for that.

Once you select your days, you want to try your best to stay on this schedule every week. Like I said, if you choose to finish your assistance work on the following day, fine. It will cost you one of your rest days, but it doesn't really matter much. The total workload is the same. Do not use this as an excuse to add some insane amount of assistance work. Pick a template, or follow the guidelines for assistance work in a custom program. *The workload must remain the same.* If you knock the scheduled session out all at once, fine. You can focus on resting or some cardio the next day. The only caveat here is that if you spit up a session, (squat and deadlift are the only two sessions difficult enough to split), you have to do the mechanically similar movement in the same session as the main movement. Do not save that for the next day. It doesn't make much sense to split up a pressing session, so I won't even get into that. If you can't finish pressing and assistance in one clip, just give up on getting strong right now. I know everyone has responsibilities outside of the gym, but the assistance work after a bench session should

Setting up your 5thSet program

take about 15 min. Just get it done and have the next day free for rest or cardio.

For the first session, the main movement of the day will be Bench Press. For the next, Squat. The third training session is a 2nd pressing day: a repetition day for upper body hypertrophy and bench assistance (though there are some other choices). On the last training session of each microcycle you will train the deadlift. These four sessions will be spread over the course of nine days.

The assistance work you do with any given session will, for the most part, be geared toward things that help the movement you performed on that day. That is not a hard and fast rule, just a logical way of setting things up. It makes sense that you would not want to be doing squat assistance work with bench press when the next session on the schedule is squat. You would be going into things already beat up and that is just not a very good strategy.

Running 5thSet

Progressions:

PROTOCOL	MESOCYCLE 1	MESOCYCLE 2	MESOCYCLE 3
Technique/ Speed	70% +5 pounds/mic	70% +5 pounds/mic	70% +5 pounds/mic
5thSet	77.5%+5 pounds/mic	80% +5 pounds/mic	80% +5 pounds/mic
Deload	50% 5 sets of 3	50% 5 sets of 3	No Deload

- Technique/Speed protocol lifts reset to 70% at the beginning of each mesocycle.
- 5thSet protocol lifts start at 77.5% for the first mesocycle and then reset to 80% for the second and third mesocycles.
- 5 pounds is added to each lift, every microcycle for 5 microcycles, then the 6th microcycle the deload protocol is performed. This completes a mesocycle.
- If you "fail-out" on one lift, do a deload microcycle for all of the lifts, reset and start a new mesocycle.
- If you manage to complete these three mesocycles without failing out, no deload will be performed on the last cycle, so that is 151 days or about five months. If you failed out, its less. Either way, it's time to do a meet and you have to go right into the 4th mesocycle, a meet prep cycle (more about this in the *"Peaking for a Meet"* section), which is designed to peak performance and only consists of 4 microcycles (36 days).

- You can simulate the circumstances of a meet and take three attempts for each lift on one day at the end of the fourth cycle, while you are peaked, if for some reason you want to train for powerlifting and not compete in it.

Weight progressions, by microcycle

Below, I have laid out an example of a specific male lifter to show you the progressions he would make each microcycle, with an overview of 3 full mesocycles. You can think of the microcycles as weeks, because that is probably how you are used to thinking about them. On 5thSet, however, a microcycle is nine days, instead of the typical seven. So, it's longer than a week and in the grand scheme of things that adds up. This is going to allow you to fit more work into each rotation and in the end, it will help you more than you know.

As you can see, this lifter has a max squat of 550 pounds, a max bench of 350 pounds and a max pull of 600 pounds. In this example, he has chosen to run the Technique/Speed protocol for deadlift and the 5thSet protocol for squat and bench. Notice that for his first mesocycle he will be starting with 77.5% for his 5thSet lifts, but for the second and third he will be starting with 80%. You might say 2.5% doesn't seem like much of a difference. Given the way we round down our figures, sometimes for lifters who are not this strong, it ends up being the same starting number for both percentages and that is fine.

Mesocycle 1

Lift	Max	%	1	2	3	4	5	6
Squat	550	77.5	425	430	435	440	445	275
Bench	350	77.5	270	275	280	285	290	175
Dead	600	70	415	420	425	430	435	300
Upper	-	N/A	-	-	-	-	-	-

Mesocycle 2

Lift	Max	%	1	2	3	4	5	6
Squat	550	80	435	440	445	450	455	275
Bench	350	80	275	280	285	290	295	175
Dead	600	70	415	420	425	430	435	300
Upper	-	N/A	-	-	-	-	-	-

Mesocycle 3

Lift	Max	%	1	2	3	4	5
Squat	550	80	435	440	445	450	455
Bench	350	80	275	280	285	290	295
Dead	600	70	415	420	425	430	435
Upper	-	N/A	-	-	-	-	-

In this case, for the first mesocycle on the the 5thSet protocol 77.5% of the lifter's 550 squat max comes out to 426.25, which we then round down to 425 pounds. For the second mesocycle 80% of 550 comes out to 440, which we round down a full five pounds to 435 pounds. So, he will be starting with ten pounds more on squat for the second and third mesocycles than he did on the first.

For his first mesocycle bench press, 77.5% of a 350-pound max comes out to 271.25, which we round down to 270 pounds. Again, for the second and third mesocycles we will use 80% which comes out to 280 and we round that down to 275 pounds.

So, this guy starts with 5 pounds more on second and third mesocycles than the first.

The deadlift is set as the Technique/Speed protocol in this example, so the figures will not vary between mesocycles. His 600-pound deadlift, starting at 70% comes out to 420, so we round that down to 415 pounds and that will be his starting weight for each of these three microcycles.

Can you switch the Technique/Speed protocol lift to squat after the first mesocycle?

Sure, if you have any reason to. If things are going well, I'd leave it alone. If you are doing a custom program, you can also change the assistance work around at that point if you want. Let's say you were smart and started with the bare minimum amount of assistance stuff. (I'm going to get into this in more detail in the custom program section.) If you seem to be recovering well enough, after that first mesocycle is when you could add a small amount to it, maybe another exercise. Or you could leave it alone. If you are following one of the templates I would not change it unless you have reason to do so. If that means it stays the same for all three mesocycles and into a meet-peaking mesocycle, so be it. If it isn't broken, don't try to fix it.

Sample program

Now, I realize that everyone learns things differently. So, I want to make sure that I show you how every part of this should look, all laid out. We've already seen nearly six months of training from an aerial view, but that didn't show what the individual training sessions actually look like in their entirety. So we will use the lifter above as an example and here is a quick look at his first microcycle:

Running 5thSet

- **Session 1**- the main lift of the day is the bench press.
- **Session 2**- the main lift of the day is the squat.
- **Session 3**- the main lift of the day is high rep wide grip bench press.
- **Session 4**- the main lift of the day is the deadlift.

Session 1- Tuesday

- **Bench Press:** 270 pounds for 4 sets of 2 reps and on his all-out 5thSet of AMRAP the lifter gets 8 reps.
- **2 Board Press:** 155 pounds for 2 sets of 15 reps. These are both easy, so the lifter makes a note to add 5 pounds to his second set next time.
- **Side Lateral Raise:** 20 pound dumbbells for 2 sets of 15 reps.
- **Rear Lateral Raise:** 15 pound dumbbells for 2 sets of 15 reps.

Session 2- Thursday

- **Squat:** 425 pounds for 4 sets of 2 reps and on his all out 5thSet the lifter gets 10 reps.
- **Reverse Hyper:** 5 sets of 10 reps. The weight was not difficult so the lifter makes a note in his book to add 10 pounds the following microcycle.
- **Barbell Rows(pronated):** 2 progressive heavy sets of 12 reps. Lifter makes a note to add 5 pounds to his second set the following microcycle.
- **Barbell Shrugs:** 2 progressive sets of 12 reps. For the first set, the lifter uses the weight that was already on the bar from his last set of rows. For the second set he adds

50 pounds. He makes a note to add 5 pounds to his second set.

Session 3- Saturday

- **Wide Grip Bench Press (2 fingers wider than competition grip):** 180 pounds for 2 sets of 25 reps. The lifter makes a note to add 5 pounds next time.
- **Rolling Tricep Extension (on the floor):** 2 progressive sets of 20 reps. The second set was not too heavy, but the lifters triceps are fried from all of the pressing. He makes a note to stick with the same weights for this movement next week.
- **Band Pull Apart:** 3 sets of 35 reps, about 60 seconds rest between. This wasn't as hard as the lifter thought it would be. He makes a note to move down the rest periods to 45 seconds next time.

Session 4- The Following Tuesday

- **Deadlift:** 415 pounds for 5 sets of 3 reps. The emphasis here is technique and speed off of the floor. Notice that the lifter does not perform an all-out 5th set for this lift, because this is the lift he has selected for the Technique/Speed protocol. He films every set from the side angle and reviews each set during his rest period, taking note of any technique issues he needs to focus on correcting in the next set. He keeps a good record of the technique issues he works on during this session so that next time he remembers to keep an eye out.
- **Rack Pulls (below the knees):** 415 pounds for 3 sets of 3 reps.

<u>The lifter didn't get much sleep the night before and is running on fumes at this point, so he decides to split the session and finish his assistance work the following day.</u>

Session 4b- Wednesday

- **Chin Ups/Pull Ups:** The lifter is careful to warm up this movement with some light pulldowns. He then performs a set of 15 pull ups followed by a set of 16 chin ups. He makes a note to add a chain over his shoulders for the next cycle, because he reached his target reps.
- **Pull Through:** 3 sets of 15 reps with a band.
- **Hammer curls:** 2 set of 20 reps.

This guy chose a Tuesday/Thursday/Saturday training schedule. Notice that the following Tuesday when he started a new week, he was still finishing his first microcycle, so he was not on the same session he did the previous Tuesday. The lifter chose to use his option to split up his assistance work for session 4. He came back on Wednesday, well rested and tore through the rest of the work. Now, on Thursday he can start a new microcycle and never miss a beat. Some people will tell you it's okay to skip assistance work, under certain circumstances. In my experience those people are not very jacked.

You probably noticed that this lifter was making a whole bunch of notes about the various things that happened during his training which pertained to the following microcycle. I'm sure you are wondering where in the hell he was making these notes. Good thinking! That's leads us to the next section.

Training Log

People look at me like I am asking them to convert to a new religion or something when I tell them they need to get a notebook and keep a training log. I am not really sure what is so difficult about this concept. Do you really think you will remember everything you do in the gym from week to week? How about what you did on your last mesocycle when you were working with the weight you are going to hit today? Are you going to memorize 30 different rep PR's?

The answer is "no" to all of these questions, so buy a notebook and keep a record of everything you do on this program. The first thing I do when someone asks me for help is say "let me see your book." By looking at a single page for 30 seconds I can see the progressions they've made on any given session for months. It's that easy for me to learn everything I need to know about what is going on to help them. When my powerlifting team is training here at Keyhole Barbell, I can have as many as 15 lifters coming up to me in the course of a session to ask for input on what is happening with their 5thSet program. This method of keeping records has proven invaluable for me, and made giving advice or feedback an almost thoughtless process.

These pictures show the way I have people set up their notebooks. I'm not going to say that this is the exact way you need to set up your training log, (you can write everything out long hand for all I care) but it has already been shown to be effective for the hundreds of lifters I have had on this program to do it this way. So, why wouldn't you do it like that? Some people love to make things difficult.

Running 5thSet

I recommend that you buy a five subject spiral notebook. It doesn't have to be anything fancy. A two dollar, five subject spiral is fine. Open to the first page in the book and use a pen to set up five columns by striking three lines, like I am doing in this picture.

The first column is the "Exercise" and the second is the "Weight" used, then "Sets" performed, then "Reps" performed, then "Notes." You will not be graded on neatness or draftsmanship.

You can fit many microcycles worth of records for this session on one page and there are enough pages in each subject to keep years worth. The first four subjects will be used for your four different sessions, respectively. For example, the picture shown below is the bench press session, the next subject would be the squat, and so on.

Running 5thSet

Exercise	Weight	Sets	Reps	Notes
Bench	160	4/1	2/7	move up
2 boards	65/135	2	15	move up
Side raise	10	2	12	
rear raise	10	2	15	
Bench	165	4/1	2/6	move up
2 boards	65/140	2	15	move up
Side raise	10	2	12	15 reps
rear raise	10	2	15	
Bench	170	4/1	2/5	move up
2 boards	65/145	2	15	move up
Side raise	10	2	15	
rear raise	10	2	15	

Before you chuckle to yourself that your 80% is higher than the figures in the book, keep in mind that this one belongs to one of my high school lifters, and she isn't very big.

Anyway, you will end up with an extra subject in the back of the book. You can't really find *four* subject spiral notebooks, unfortunately. Use the left-over subject to write down your deepest personal thoughts, or draw sketches of people you hate, on fire. Apparently, that is what she does.

Peaking for a Meet

I've noticed a trend in powerlifting, now that many lifters video their training and post it on social media as they prepare for a meet. It is possible that this has been happening all along, and it's just the posting of videos that brought it to my attention, but I feel like the videos themselves have had some impact on it. It's another thing that causes me to shake my head, like so many of the easily avoidable disappointments I have mentioned in this book. A lifter will hit huge PR's in training to post the videos of it on social media, then perform poorly in their meet, hitting lower numbers than they did in training.

Now, it's possible that the lifter actually got sick, or pulled a muscle or whatever other likely-bullshit excuse was given. Things do go terribly wrong sometimes, I know firsthand. I've dropped the bar on myself during bench press, which not only cost me that lift, but severely herniated my L5-S1 and definitely took the wind out of my sails for deadlift. That's not what I'm referring to here. I'm talking about the lifter who, on meet day, just isn't there. The guy from the YouTube videos is nowhere in sight and he's been replaced with some clown who is grinding out an opener 30 pounds less than what was in his last video.

So, the question here is "What went wrong?" What are all of these lifters doing wrong that is causing them to miss their maximal attempts the only time they really matter? The answer is either that they are peaking too soon or using a program with no regard for peaking whatsoever.

When using the 5thSet program, peaking too soon is not an option. You are ready to peak for a meet within 36 days from *any point* in your training (once you have completed your first mesocycle) and being on a rigid program like this keeps you from doing any dumb shit. Let's say you get a last-minute opportunity that you really don't want to pass up, to compete in a big meet which is only 28 days from now. Can you make it work and peak in time for that meet? Absolutely. You have some leeway with the peaking cycle. Here is how it works.

At about 36 days out from your meet you are going to start a microcycle which will be identical to the one you've just completed, except that, instead of your normal percentages, you are going to be working up to a training max for each of the competition lifts on their respective sessions. You do not want to fail, but you want to get as close as you possibly can to a 100% 1RM for that day, which means taking smaller jumps when things get heavy.

If you have to get started on your peaking cycle right away and you are still mid-microcycle, you can just start your maxes with the next scheduled lift and roll with maxes until you've done all four sessions. Your MSM's will be moved up to 75% and the rep scheme will move down to 3-5 reps. Your 2nd pressing day will stay the same as normal. The next cycle through, you are going to hit all competition lifts for at least 90% of the 100% maxes you just tested, use "press" and "rack" commands for bench and your assistance work and MSM's will remain the same, but your 2nd pressing day's main lift will be performed with lowered weight. Next, on the third microcycle you will perform the lifts with 80% for one set of three reps. On bench press you will pause every rep and practice following the "press" and "rack" commands, even in the heavier warm ups. For this microcycle you will reduce the weights on your assistance work, but keep the reps how they've been. If you started this peaking mesocycle with less than 36 days left before the meet, cut the additional days from this, *the third* microcycle. On the fourth and final microcycle of your meet peaking mesocycle, you will perform all three competition lifts on the same day, with no assistance work, six days prior to the meet. For all of the lifts you will use 55% of the recently established 1RM, moving the bar as quickly as possible. Squats will be performed for 5 sets of 2 reps. Bench press will be performed for 5 sets of 3 reps and deadlift will be performed for 5 singles. From six days out you will not touch a barbell until the meet. Selecting openers and all attempts for that matter will be covered in the "Meet Day" section, in detail.

Peak Schedule

Your meet-peaking mesocycle is going to look something like this:

- Microcycle 1 – find 100% max single for each lift, full assistance work, 75% for MSM's for 3-5 reps.
- Microcycle 2 – work up to, or slightly above 90% of the previous microcycle for a single, commands for benches, full assistance, 75% for MSM's for 3-5 reps.
- Microcycle 3 – 80% for a triple, commands for benches, all assistance weights lowered.
- Microcycle 4 – 55% for speed work - 6 days before meet, no assistance.
    - Squat – 5 sets of 2 reps
    - Bench – 5 sets of 3 reps
    - Deadlift – 5 singles

The closer you stick to these guidelines, the better your rebound will be in peaking your strength for meet day. Increases of 4-5% from the maxes that you hit during this cycle are not uncommon, when peaked properly for a meet. In fact, with my lifters, I count on it. Generally, lifters with better overall recoverability tend to get even larger rebounds when peaking, but I almost always stick to these figures. The logic is that most lifters will go 9 for 9 with this system and end up leaving less on the platform than if they take more risky attempts and miss. In other words, this system will produce the highest possible total in the vast majority of cases.

An Important Note on The Peaking Cycle:

This phase is not the payoff for your training. I want to be clear about that. This is a ***death march***. This is you, still earning the dividends that will be paid to you on the platform. There may be times during the first microcycle that you are disappointed about your performance. You expected more. That is normal. You have to keep giving your all and have faith in the process. Do not expect your reward yet. There is a long-term delay to the training effect. Once you've done a few meets with this method you will understand the role of this cycle better. Do not get downhearted when you don't hit huge PRs. That is what needs to be done at the meet.

You are fatigued going into this. I want you to murder yourself in the pursuit of the best number possible for the first microcycle, but do not be surprised or discouraged when that number is not as high as you would like. It isn't time for that yet. That time is coming. Now is the time to harden up, hold it together and work.

Meet Day

The day of the meet is something that can be really difficult for people who don't have a lot of experience with competition or can't handle pressure well. Everyone reacts to it in their own way. I've worked with people who, based on their demeanor, aren't impacted by it at all. I've also worked with people who get so worked up and nervous that they end up running outside to vomit up their breakfast. Myself, I fall somewhere in between. I get very quiet. I am in my head, visualizing. I don't want to talk until it's done, until I have a decent squat opener on the books. That's something I find is pretty universal. Once a lifter is able to get an opener on the books and passed, all the tension is broken. From there, things get a lot easier, no matter who you are. If this is your first meet, adjust the figures my formula will give you down a bit.

With everything that's going on and the fact that you have probably trained for the last 3-6 months in preparation for the nine attempts you get to take on this one day, the last thing you want to have to worry about is figuring out a strategy for selecting your attempts. This is where having a coach is awesome, because you can just sit back and relax and, when you are in the hole, get ready to take your attempt. Well, since you are doing my program, let me be your coach.

I have developed a system based off of the training maxes you take during the meet peaking cycle, which makes selecting attempts for the meet a thoughtless endeavor. This is what I use for all of my lifters and so if I was working with you, this is most likely how I would come up with your attempts for meet day.

Before I show you my formula for selecting attempts I want to offer a word of caution. For a lifter who is new to competition, there is no suitable replacement for an experienced coach. That's the truth. I can give you these figures and they are excellent guidelines. In fact, 99% of the time I stick to the formula or within 1% of it. I am closely monitoring the training leading up to these meets, though. I know how these people lift. Some decisions have to be made "on the fly" by someone with an experienced eye. If you feel you are experienced enough to do that for yourself, fine.

Also, I have to tell you that if anything went wrong when you were taking your training maxes during your meet peaking cycle and those maxes were not accurate and near 100%, this formula will not work and the figures you come up with will be worthless. These things happen. In that case you want to have someone with experience to call your numbers for you, preferably someone who knows your lifting. If that is not possible and you don't have the experience to make the tough calls yourself, have fun with it. This is a hobby and it's supposed to be fun. There is time to become a world champion down the road. Open light, with a lift you can do for an easy triple and throw a little weight on for your next attempt. Make the most of the day.

With all of that said, never in my life have I not lifted more in a meet that I did in my training for that meet (barring catastrophe). Never have I coached a lifter who did a peaking phase and didn't hit a larger number in the meet than they did in their training for the meet. Here is how we make that happen:

Meet Day

Attempt #	Multiplication Coefficient
1	0.9
2	0.97
3	1.02-1.04

Multiply the maxes from your meet peaking cycle by the coefficient listed for each attempt in the table above. It's a good idea to do this ahead of time, so you don't need to worry about it at the meet. Everything gets rounded down to the nearest increment of five pounds. If something looks much harder than it should in the meet, you can adjust your next attempt accordingly. If you do everything correctly, you shouldn't have to.

Sample attempt selection

To give an example of how this should work let's say that a lifter comes up with 600 pounds as a max during their peaking cycle for squat. In this case the lifter would multiply 600 x 0.9 to calculate the opening attempt for that lift. 600 x 0.9 = 540 so the lifter's opener would be 540 pounds. To calculate the second attempt the lifter would multiply 600 x 0.97, which equals 582, rounded down, 580 pounds. Simple enough. Now for the third, the lifter would consider how fast the bar moved or how difficult the second attempt was. Reviewing a video of the second attempt is an invaluable help, assisting in this decision. If the second looked harder than it should've, you're going to have to use your best judgment. If the lift looked smooth and the lifter was able to drive right through it, I would still err on the side of caution and go with 1.04 as the coefficient for the third attempt. 1.05 is reserved for times when the lifter's second attempt was an absolute joke in regard to effort, like the weight just flew up. So, let's go with the "middle of the road" scenario, 600 x 1.04 =

Meet Day

624 pounds, which we would round down to 620 pounds for the lifter's third attempt.

So, for this lifter's squat attempts we come up with:

- 1st attempt- 600 x 0.9 = 540 pounds.
- 2nd attempt- 600 x 0.97 = 580 pounds. (582 rounded down)
- 3rd attempt- 600 x 1.04 = 620 pounds. (624 rounded down)

This formula is then used for your deadlift in the same manner and hopefully you PR on every lift, PR on your total, fall in love with your soulmate, inherit a bunch of money from a family member you've never met and spend the rest of your life on a yacht, cruising around the south pacific islands.

Bench Press Attempt Selection:

The release of the first 5thSet book allowed me to gather a tremendous amount of data from the thousands of lifters who went on to use the program. In a single year I was able to collect more meet results from 5thSet lifters than the entire ten years prior. This has really allowed me to fine tune the formula for attempt selection. Most of this data simply confirmed what we already knew, but one significant deviation should not be overlooked. More third attempt bench presses were missed than any other lift. By changing the third attempt multiplication coefficient from 1.04 to 1.02 this has been corrected. 102.5% can be used in cases where the lifter's second attempt looked exceptionally easy.

Meet Day

A few more key points of advice I want to touch on regarding meet day:

- **Stay Hydrated-** drink plenty of water from the minute you get up on the day of your meet. Continue to sip water and Gatorade throughout the whole day, especially if you use stimulants, because these drugs can act as diuretics. Dehydration can greatly increase the likelihood of an injury.

- **Have Something in Your Stomach-** notice that I said *IN* your stomach, meaning you want it to stay there. If you are someone who gets very nervous you might have a hard time keeping down a hearty breakfast of pancakes and eggs and so on. I know more than one person like this. Even though it might temporarily relieve your anxiety to stuff your face, it can't help you if you don't keep it down. Personally, I just do not have much of an appetite at "go time." I'm just ready to get to work and get under the bar, so, food is the last thing on my mind. Regardless of how you feel, the fact is that everyone performs better with some calories in them. I like to have a shake with 50 grams of protein and 100 grams of carbs in the morning before warming up squats. (I'm almost 300 pounds.) It is convenient, and easy for me to digest. The shake not having any fat in it speeds gastric emptying, which helps any meet day supplements (ergogenic aids, etc.) to kick in quickly. (Don't learn the hard way how fast things get moving at an early morning meet.) If you don't lift until the afternoon, this part is less crucial. You will perform better with calories in you. Keep reminding yourself.

- **Warm Up Well for Squats-** the vast majority of pulled muscles and minor injuries I have seen at powerlifting meets have happened during the squat and if I had to venture a guess as to why that is, I would say a combination of insufficient hydration and not being warmed up thoroughly for max attempts. Getting hurt during squat is a sure way to stack the cards against yourself for the rest of the meet. Any time you get under that bar to take an attempt you are risking getting hurt. Do everything in your power to prevent it. Show up to the meet on time so that you can pace yourself through warm ups. Treat it like the beginning of a training session. Stretch out. Do some warm ups for your trunk. Squat the bar a whole bunch. Take small jumps with lighter weights and just keep the reps low. Sip fluids between sets.

- **When You Are Not Lifting, Be Resting-** even meets that run like clockwork can span the entire day if there are enough competitors. Waiting around and stressing about when you are up will sap your strength. Once you are told to warm up for your flight, do it. If they aren't announcing that info, ask the meet director approximately when your flight will be. Until then, find a place to sit and relax. When the warm ups for your flight come and you are all done warming up, find someplace close enough to the platform to set up so you can clearly hear who is "on deck" and "in the hole." Between attempts, clear your mind and think only about the lift you are about to perform. Visualize the bar moving smoothly. Do not stress.

- **Show Sportsmanship-** if you miss a lift due to being red lighted, do not act like an asshole. You have every right to ask a judge their reasoning for giving you a red light, but whether or not you agree, their opinion is what matters and you have to respect it. It is okay to be angry, but show sportsmanship. Keep in mind that two judges had to agree you did something illegal for the lift not to pass. If you have another attempt left, come back and make it perfect. If not, keep your head high and take it on the chin.

After the Meet (What Now?)

Powerlifters have a tendency to act like mental patients in the weeks following a meet. They are typically moody and emotional, sad, or just plain miserable (here's the thing) even when they perform really well in the meet. Of course, not everyone is effected by this phenomenon, but in my experience the majority of us are, at least to some degree. And it is understandable, I mean, you spend months and months with one goal in mind; you toil, resolute, in preparation for it. This destination becomes your purpose. Once you finally reach it, that goal; even if everything goes as planned and you win the day, after a moment's rejoice; after an evening of celebration: something begins to grow inside of you. It is a kind of awareness that your once purposeful existence has become less so. What now? What do you focus on, now that the thing you've pursued with such obstinate resolve is so decidedly in your rear view? I guess you could turn to religion for purpose, or try to dull things a bit with alcohol. Some people do alright with those.

I prefer to get right back to business.

Now, your body is beyond taxed at this point, probably more beat up than it felt at any point in the preceding training cycles. So what, do you take a week or two off?

No. That is not the best idea in my experience. You've already backed way off on your assistance work and training volume for the last weeks before the meet. More time completely off from training results in a really difficult transition back, once you do start. But, you are really not ready to train, you might be thinking, and you'd be correct. So, what to do? Don't worry we have a plan for that, too. Below is what I have found to be the most effective way to transition back into training the 5thSet program after a meet.

After the Meet (What Now?)

Take at least a full day off after the meet. Then, on your next scheduled training day, start a microcycle to bridge from the meet into your new mesocycle. This microcycle will not count toward your coming mesocycle, but rather it is like a preparatory recovery phase. Spread the workouts out the way you would normally, over the next nine days. You will simply be going through the frame work of the program. For all three lifts you will use 35% of your 1RM and perform three sets of five reps. For assistance work, you will use weights which are easy and go through everything with the standard set and rep schemes you would usually use. On the 2nd pressing day, 35% of 1RM or approximately 2/3 of normal starting weight for the main movement will be used for the normal target number of repetitions.

For example, if you are doing wide grip bench press and your bench max is 500 pounds, 35% rounded down is 170 pounds. If incline dumbbell is your main movement for high reps and you would be starting your cycle with 100 pound dumbbells, you would use 65's. Start a new mesocycle after you've completed this recovery microcycle, using the max lifts from your meet peaking phase, before the meet. It is probably not the best idea to use your meet lifts as a training max.

So, your meet-recovery microcycle is going to look something like this:

- Main Movements- Squat, Bench, Deadlift
    - Performed as usual in their respective sessions.
    - 35% of 1RM is used.
    - 3 sets of 5 repetitions are performed.
    - 2nd Pressing Day 35% 1RM or 2/3 starting weight is used for high rep scheme.
- Assistance work

- - o Easy weights for every exercise.
  - o Normal set and rep schemes.
- When you finish the recovery microcycle: start a new mesocycle.

This is pretty simple stuff. Doing a cycle like this will help you recover more quickly than doing nothing at all, and it will help preserve certain capacities which would suffer otherwise. Most lifters I work with are able to mitigate the post-meet bullshit by getting right back on track with these guidelines. I've seen people who just decide to wing it after a meet go off the rails wildly. It helps to have a plan and this is a solid one.

Building a Custom 5thSet Program

For those of you who choose to put together your own 5thSet program: below you will find an almost fool proof guide to programming assistance work. Once you have selected which of the main lifts will be your technique/speed protocol lift or lifts, all that remains in building your custom program is selecting your assistance work. You can choose to program assistance work for each day or just certain days. It's entirely up to you. (Again, if this is going to be the first time you use this program, do yourself a favor and pick a template.)

I'm going to give you a lot of freedom to choose from a variety of exercises and protocols and I encourage you to try a variety of things to see what works best for you. **Start with the bare minimum for the first cycle of your custom program.** If this works well for you, stick with it. If you feel like you are recovering alright and want to add a movement to the next cycle, go ahead. Some advice: whatever you try, *stick with it for at least a full training cycle*. Like I said, if it is working well and you are making progress, don't change it. If you get stuck, try changing *one thing*, not the whole deal. It's very hard to figure out what is working if you change too many things at once.

You can try doing less than the framework I've recommended, but in most cases it is not a good idea to do more. Take this to heart or you will be humbled in the middle of a training cycle.

Notice the conspicuous absence of such popular muscle magazine methods as "running the rack style drop-sets." I have not found these methods to be effective in my own experience and for our purposes they are illogical. For one, it's very difficult to quantify the amount of work done with multi-stage drop sets, because there are so many variables. So when the time comes to add, correct or modify the workload in any way it's almost impossible to do so effectively. Most of this stuff just complicates what should be a very simple thing.

It's assistance work, that's all. For the most part, we are just trying to add muscle or strength to the areas that will be most effective in assisting the lifts. This is not the science of rockets.

If you aren't sure what your weak points are, at some point when you take a max, video the lift. Watch it again and again. Try to see if you can spot where things started to go wrong. If you get the bar 8" off of your chest before failing on bench press, you need to work on lock out and your exercise selection should reflect that. In the meantime, just work on adding size and strength to your whole body with basic movements.

Mechanically Similar Movement (MSM)

Pay attention to this part. MSM's are intrinsic to the 5thSet program. A Mechanically Similar Movement (MSM) is a movement that looks like a certain phase of the main lift you are training on a given day, or any compound, multi-joint movement that is similar to a main lift in its entirety. Your most important assistance exercise of the day will usually be a mechanically similar movement, performed with a hypertrophy based set and rep scheme most times, or in some cases a heavier strength based set and rep scheme, focused on a relative weak point. (You may, in some cases, want to substitute a multi-joint movement that is not similar to the main movement, such as pull ups. Doing both is fine, also.) Mechanically similar exercises should be performed first in your assistance work, immediately after the main lift of the day. If you only do one assistance exercise per training session, it should be one of these. An exception would be that you need to do back exercises like rows or pull ups with squat and deadlift sessions even if you do not also do an MSM. Most lifters will do both. And don't forget: splitting up the assistance and finishing the next day is an option.

Some examples of exercises which are good to use as **Mechanically Similar Movements (MSM)** would be *rack pulls below the knees* performed *after* your deadlift work for the day, or a *2 board press* *after* your bench press work for the day. I do not think training certain phases of the lift for squat is your best bet for MSM's. Instead pick a full range lift that targets the lagging muscle group. A good example would be a *front squat or SSB squat* *after* your back squat if the quadriceps are lagging. I'm going to include a short list of these for you to choose from for each lift, but feel free to try new things. With that said, once you pick a movement, give it time to work. I say that again and again: it bears repeating.

You get a little freedom (a few options, rather) for your set and rep schemes, too. Basically, what it boils down to is that you will choose whether the goal should be to use an assistance exercise to build muscle (for this you would choose the **hypertrophy protocol**), or to focus more on building strength in a particular phase of the lift, or even peaking closer to a meet (you would choose the **strength protocol** for those).

Hypertrophy Protocol:

For hypertrophy, you would perform three to five sets of ten to fifteen repetitions. The first set should be a weight which is moderately heavy, like an RPE(Rate of Perceived Exertion) of 4. The RPE scale is used to measure the intensity of exercise and it runs from 0-10. "0" would be sitting around on the couch and "10" is very, very heavy. If a butterfly landed on the bar while you were doing a single with an RPE of 10, you would miss the lift. So "10" is the way you feel after doing an exercise stress test, basically like you're going to fall down and die. An RPE of 4 is somewhat heavy. You will move the weight up for the following set and stick with that weight for the remaining sets, regardless of how many you do. Your second and all remaining sets will be performed with a weight which is an RPE of about 6 for you (heavy, but not very heavy). Use these weights for the first session and you will gradually move up the weight for these sets throughout the training cycle.

Forty to fifty total reps is a good number for a hypertrophy exercise. You want to include a compound, multi-joint movement with the hypertrophy protocol for lats in your deadlift session and your squat session. I've found it works best to do a rowing movement like barbell rows or chest supported rows on the squat day and pull ups/chin ups with deadlifts, though there are some other ways you could do this.

Strength Protocol:

To strengthen a weak point in the lift, (for example, lockout) you would do something more along the lines of 2-3 sets of 3-5 reps starting with around 70% of your full range 1RM for the lift. For a Weighted Chin or a Front Squat, examples of movements which actually are full range, you would take a rep max and use the coefficient chart I gave you to find the 1RM and use 70% of that number.

Again, you would gradually add weight to this over the course of the training cycle. 6-15 total reps is reasonable volume for this protocol, but start on the low end of that. This option is usually going to be used after the main lift on your 70% day. The emphasis on that day is technical correction and speed with a lower percentage, so this is an ideal day to add some harder assistance work after the main lift.

A point of advice: for the days you are doing your 80% 5thSet lifts, stick with the hypertrophy protocol, most of the time. Remember it is possible to over-do assistance work and while it can be important, nothing should ever interfere with the main lifts. If you are doing lower rep, high intensity assistance work for everything you'll get beat up and burn out quick.

An example of a time when it would be advisable to use the strength protocol for an assistance exercise on an 80% 5thSet day would be the first couple of microcycles on the meet/peaking mesocycle. Lowering the volume and increasing intensity can help during this period. Another example would be if you kept the total assistance volume very low on an 80% day anyway. Say, if you were to only do one assistance exercise, maybe two.

The second type of exercise you can use for assistance work is going to be an isolation movement. This is generally the least effective type of exercise and for this reason I do not usually waste my time doing many of them. However, when performed after your main lift and a mechanically similar assistance movement (or any multi joint movement), isolation exercises can help bring up a weak or lagging body part. These should be performed for around the high end of the total target reps you would use for the above hypertrophy protocol. You can feel free to try them with the set and rep scheme outlined. However, I have found some of these movements to work best with very high reps per set. Let's say 20-30 for 1-2 sets. Either way pick a set and rep scheme and stick with it for a while.

Some examples of good choices for this type of movement would be **hammer curls** for biceps, **standing calf raises** for calves, over or underhand **cable extensions** or **rolling dumbbell extensions** for triceps. **side lateral raise** for deltoids, **rear lateral raise**, **band pull aparts** or **face pulls** for rear deltoids and the scapular muscles, **leg curls** for hamstrings, barbell or db **shrugs** for traps, even **weighted crunches** for abs or **toes to bar** (if you are that zealous).

The 2nd pressing day:

For the second pressing day in the 5thSet program, it is business as usual in regards to the order of operation. You still have a main movement on this day. The main movement is still a relatively heavy compound lift and it is still always performed first. The objective here is to pick a type of press and and train it with a very high rep scheme (25-35 reps). I've seen these work wonders for people who just cant seem to develop a good bench press. That is because most of those people lack the amount of muscular development necessary to stabilize heavy weights and this will certainly help with that. There is a list about a mile long of options you could pick for this lift, but only two that you will ever really need.

1. **Wide Grip Barbell Bench Press**: These do not need to be excessively wide. Just move 2 finger widths out from your competition grip, if possible. If you use pinkies on the ring for your competition grip, put middle fingers on the ring for this. I've seen these work best for 1-2 working sets of 25 reps after warming up. Whenever you reach your target reps, add five pounds the following week. 50-52.5% of 1RM for bench is a good place to start these. I like to do 3 warm up sets of 15 reps with light weight.

2. **Incline Dumbbell Press**: I prefer to do these with a neutral, palms facing grip, but they work great either way. These are best done for 2 working sets in the 30-35 rep range. The first week your sets should be difficult but not murder. Eventually they will be murder. Move up by five when you reach target reps.

5thSet custom program recap:

MAIN LIFT
MSM
ISOLATION MOVEMENT

That is pretty simple stuff, right? Like I said, not the science of rockets. Keep in mind that you don't have to do one of each type of assistance movement with each training session. In fact, for your first custom program cycle I do not recommend it. You don't even have to put assistance work on the schedule for every training session if you don't want, but remember: whatever you decide, stick to the plan.

The Competition Lifts

Powerlifting is a fairly simple sport. Strategy can be a little bit complex and not everyone can agree on the best way to prepare for competition, but the sport itself is about as easy of a concept to grasp as I can imagine. You can bring a person to a meet who has no prior knowledge of how things work and in very few words explain everything they need to know about the contest they are going to watch.

The competitors will perform the squat, the bench press and the deadlift, and get three progressive attempts for each. Once an attempt has been taken, the bar weight can only go up or stay the same for subsequent attempts. The heaviest attempt successfully completed in each lift will go towards the lifter's total; so, their heaviest squat, bench press, and deadlift will constitute their "total." The lifter with the heaviest total wins.

That is about all you need to know to watch a powerlifting meet and get what is going on: four sentences. This emphasizes the actual importance of the competition lifts, they are the whole sport. It goes without saying that for a top-level competitor, a technical mastery of these three lifts is absolutely paramount.

The best way to master the lifts is to learn first how to perform them correctly. Working, hands on and in person, with an experienced coach is definitely the easiest way to learn the lifts and perfect your technique, but that technique can only be solidified through practice, lots of practice. And as you practice you will need to correct form when it begins to degrade, which it will over time.

 For this reason, I recommend that everyone video all of their working sets in training and correct any issues in real time, before things get bad, whenever possible.

The Competition Lifts

The Squat (mid-bar)

- Grip the bar as narrow as your shoulder mobility will allow, but not inside of elbows.

- Ideal bar placement varies from person to person, but the majority of raw powerlifters benefit from a mid-bar position, somewhere between low bar and high bar. This is a point to go over with a coach.

- Keep shoulder blades retracted and depressed (pinched together and pulled down).

- Take a stance that puts your heels at shoulder width apart or slightly wider.

- Turn your chest up hard, brace your core and overfill your lungs. Hold your breath and bear down the whole time the bar is moving. You can stop and breathe at the top.

- Squeeze the bar, but do not press into it with your arms or pull down on it at any point during the squat. Your upper back supports the bar, not your arms.

- Keep your chest up, back flat, and torso somewhat upright throughout the movement.

- Force your knees apart as you near the bottom; continue until the crease of your hip is below the top surface of your knee.

- Drive your elbows forward and your upper back into the bar as you drive your feet (mid-foot to heel) into the floor on the way up.

The Competition Lifts
The Bench Press

- The best hand position for the bench press is another thing that varies from person to person, depending mostly on the width of a lifters shoulders. Impingement and other shoulder joint issues can sometimes be mitigated by taking a more narrow grip, while a wider grip will shorten the lift's range of motion, which can be a plus. The majority of raw powerlifters will benefit from a "pinkies on the ring" or wider grip, but there is a lot of variance here. This should also be discussed with a coach.
- Grab the bar at the desired grip position, hands even, based on the knurling.
- Slide your body back until your sternum is under the bar and pull yourself up to sit on the bench with your chest behind the bar in the rack.

The Competition Lifts

- Plant your feet in a position so that when you slide back down the bench your feet will be somewhat behind your knees.

- Slide back down, retract and depress your shoulder blades, arch your mid-back, bury the top of your traps into the pad of the bench, and do not let your feet slide forward. This will feel tight on your hips and very uncomfortable. If it isn't uncomfortable you are either a gymnast, or you are doing it wrong.
- Tighten your back and abdominal muscles and glutes, then drive your feet. Fill your lungs, and bear down.
- Keep your shoulder blades back and down as you remove the bar from the rack.

- Lower the bar until it touches your chest. Do not lift your head off of the bench.

- Bar placement will vary: lower on the abdomen for a wide grip and just under the pecs or breasts for a more narrow grip. However you grip the bar, touch where your *elbows line up in the same plane, vertically under your wrists* and make sure bar placement is consistent for each rep.

- Keep your shoulder blades back and drive your feet as you press. Lock out every rep.

The Deadlift (Conventional)

- Set yourself up so that the center line of each foot is directly under the bar, toes in front, heels behind; toes slightly further apart than heels.

- The best width for your feet varies based on a lot of factors, but the majority of raw lifters benefit from a narrower than shoulder width foot placement. You need to play with this and see what works best as far keeping your lower back arched or flat at the very least.

- Reach down and grab the bar with a mixed grip (one hand over, one hand under).

- Grip width should be outside of your thighs. Some people benefit from a grip as close to their legs as possible. I need to grip a little wider to set my shoulders correctly. You'll need to play with this, too.

- Do not allow the bar to roll out of position.

- Flatten your back, straighten your legs somewhat and tighten them.
- Tighten your abs and low back, then fill your whole midsection with air before pushing your hips back to load your hamstrings.
- Lower your hips and turn up your chest, retracting and depressing your shoulder blades. The top of your shoulder blades should be over the bar as you lean back to start the pull.
- I like to pull the slack out of the bar and think about driving my feet (the back half of each foot) into the floor as hard as I can, using my quads to get the bar moving, and once its moving I try to accelerate by following through and driving my hips forward to lock it out as urgently as possible.
- Lower the bar to the floor, under control, and reset for every rep. Do not ever drop the bar at the top of a deadlift unless it falls out of your hands.
- Do not perform touch-and-go reps. They interfere with the self-regulating mechanism of this program and generally speaking, the carryover into your 1RM is just not on par with dead stop reps. They are fine for hypertrophy, if you use a weight you can handle and stay under control **and you are not doing this program**. It's worth mentioning that watching someone perform touch and go reps with over 80% of their 1RM for AMRAP is usually not going to be pretty.

The Competition Lifts

The Deadlift (Sumo)

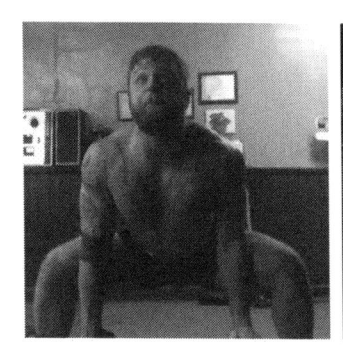

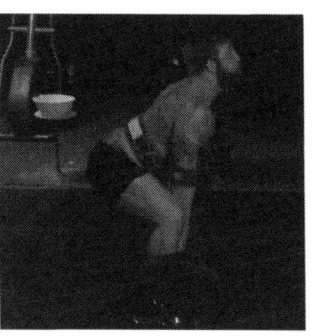

Mike Rivi forces his knees apart and braces his mid-section with a neutral spine; his foot placement has his shins vertical as he initiates the pull.

- Position in relation to the bar is very important for this type of deadlift.

- Foot placement is an individual thing and can vary greatly from lifter to lifter. It can mean the difference between not being able to lift very much and pulling a PR.

- A closer stance typically helps get the bar moving more easily, a wider stance gives an advantage at lockout.

- In most cases an ultra-wide sumo stance is not advantageous for raw powerlifters.

- A good general rule when deciding foot width is to choose the width which has the shins as close to vertical as possible when you force your knees out to initiate the lift.

- For most raw powerlifters "toes out" works best for sumo. Keeping the feet too straight tends to grind the hips. Set them at around 45 degrees and adjust from there.

- Start by getting your hips as close to the bar as possible. This means you wont drop them as much as you could. If you start with them too low, they will just shoot up anyway.

- Force your knees apart, brace your lower back and tighten your midsection before filling your lungs with air. Drive the center of your foot into the ground with your chest turned up, over the bar.

- Try to lock out your knees as quickly as possible, staying upright and following through with your hips.

How to warm up

I will just start by laying out some common sense here. It is a good idea to start out every training session with a general warm up. Even five to ten minutes on a treadmill or stationary bike can help prepare your body for the work ahead. Once you have done that, some stretching is not a bad idea. At that point I usually move on to some stability exercises for my core. I realize you might not have much time to spend in the gym, but this stuff takes fifteen minutes or less if you move through it with purpose. Remember that when you are in the gym, you are on the clock. You are there for one reason: to do work. Not to talk to your friends and joke around, not to look at your phone and play on the internet: **work.** Something I cannot stand is people claiming they don't have time to warm up correctly and then half way through their training they take a twenty minute break to text or talk to other people in the gym. Do not be one of those people.

A general warm up can help prevent injuries and improve your performance under the bar. There is a lot of room to modify this routine, but to give you an idea of what a reasonable general warm up looks like I will lay out *my own* typical warm up:

The Competition Lifts

- Seven minutes on the stationary bike or five minutes on the elliptical.
- A small amount of shoulder mobility work and lower body stretching.
- Bird Dogs, Ab Wheel and Side Bridges, to warm up the muscles I use to brace.

During this time I am typically sipping coffee or finishing my pre-workout shake between warm ups and being intermittently assailed by reports from the various lifters on my team about how their elbow or shoulder or back hurts. I consider that my psychological warm up.

Above: (left) The Side Bridge, (right) The Bird Dog

The next order of business from here is to warm up the main lift of the day, or the specific warm up. My basic recommendations for a specific warm up are that you start with the bar and perform at least 2 sets of at least 8 reps with it. For weaker lifters (example: a 125 pound max) this can be taxing and in that case you start with sets of 5 reps. I use this as an opportunity to go over my cues for the lift I am doing, in my head.

The Competition Lifts

If it's bench press I will be thinking of chesting-up to the bar as I bring it down, using my lats to stabilize the descent and really contracting them. I will do a very high number of reps and bring the bar in and out of the rack with my elbows locked, again and again. If I'm squatting I might be thinking about consciously keeping my core very tight throughout the movement or forcing my knees out in the hole. You get the idea. Obviously it's difficult to warm up the deadlift using only the bar, because the plates typically set the bar height, so make sure you do a good warm up for your core on this day. Weaker lifters can warm up using smaller plates and pulling from mats, or using bumper plates.

Once you are done with the bar, it's best to move on with progressive triples up to your working weight for the day. Again, I am going over the cues for that lift in my head as I warm up. I visualize my working sets moving quickly. Every warm up set is preparing me both mentally and physically to perform at my absolute best with my weight for the day.

I recommend at least three progressions for your three to five rep warm ups, but five progressions is a better idea. Something like 30%x5, 40%x3, 50%x3, 60%x3, 70%x3 is probably ideal. Keep the warm ups at three reps or less from 50% on. If you feel better doing more warm up sets, do more. If you find doing too much before your working sets wears you out, keep them lighter, and on the heavier warm ups do less reps. You need to experiment and find out what works best for you, but I do not recommend you try doing the working sets with any less than three progressive warm ups first and *always hit the bar a couple of times to get started.* (I'm talking about the barbell, never drink before you train.)

Gear check

As a raw powerlifter, the amount of gear you are going to need to train in will be minimal. These are a few things that will help you perform your best and could possibly prevent some training related injuries.

Footwear

You need shoes. They do not need to be fancy. Anything with a non-compressible sole will do. If you choose to buy a pair of "lifters" or olympic lifting shoes to squat in, that is fine, but first make sure you will benefit from a lifted heel! If you are someone who has an issue with coming forward on the squat, an elevated heel is going to make that worse and you'd be better off squatting in something with a flat sole. Personally, I love squatting in Adidas Adipower weightlifting shoes and sometimes I will bench in them, too. They have an aggressive lift, but that works well for me. Pretty much no one benefits from deadlifting in a shoe with an elevated heel except for maybe as a variation in training. Some people will claim that they do, but I can't see how it does anything but make the lift more difficult.

Lifting Belt

I trained and competed for many years without a belt. If I am being honest, this started because the belt I had when I started lifting was ridiculous looking and I was embarrassed to put it on. The result was that I developed a tremendously strong mid-section and really learned how to use it, early in the game. For this reason, I always have new lifters start without a belt until we are able to develop a good base and teach them how to use their core correctly. Though I wear one now, I have pulled well over 700 pounds without a belt. These are all points to consider when

Gear check

deciding whether or not to wear a belt in your training. I am not comfortable recommending that someone lift without a belt who is not working with me directly. It's important to consider that you are allowed to wear a belt in any division for raw powerlifting, it can help you prevent an injury and it can improve your performance, absolutely. I recommend a 13mm or ½" x 4" single prong style power belt.

Wrist Wraps

Learn from my mistakes and use wrist wraps. Take my advice on this. I have always been a minimalist when it comes to supportive gear. If I could not get the lift on my own, I didn't want to get it. While the idea was noble, the reality of dropping well over 500 pounds on my chest more than once (one time with 550 pounds) was harrowing. Before you say that you've benched that much without wraps and didn't drop it: so did I, hundreds of times. Dropping it twice was enough for me to re-think things and once should have been. Exactly nobody is impressed by you lifting without wrist wraps and if you ever get strong enough to lift big weights, the extra stability they provide could save your life. Just a thought.

Another point I want to touch on is wearing wrist wraps for the squat. Beyond the obvious relief they provide your wrists and protection from the torque they absorb throughout the lift, I've found wrist wraps to be extremely helpful in alleviating some other pain lifters experience from squatting: elbow and shoulder pain. I have an idea about how this works, but the bottom line is *it does work*. The logical line of reasoning is that the wrists are the weakest link in the chain when it comes to holding the bar on your back during a squat. If you squat without wrist wraps, you know that the torque on your wrists can be sometimes unbearable and this is especially true for larger lifters with limited shoulder mobility. As a result it is an almost involuntary reaction

Gear check

for your elbows and shoulders to compensate and try to remove some of the strain from your wrists. The result is pain everywhere instead of just pain in your wrists. Now the list of possible causes of shoulder and elbow pain is "holy shit" long, so this is not some cure-all solution, but it does eliminate one possible culprit and reduce the stress on those areas.

There are a lot of good reasons to wear wrists wraps. What reason could you possibly have not to? You don't have twenty bucks? There is really not much of a decision to make here. Buy them and wear them. I recommend 60cm for beginners and women, and 80cm for men. My preference is the EliteFTS Super Heavy wrist wrap, but start with something lighter.

Knee Sleeves

This is a matter of personal preference for the raw squatter. I tried a couple of different pairs of knee sleeves in the old days and never really felt comfortable in them. So, when I was younger I always squatted without sleeves. As I got older, after sixteen years or so of squatting, my knees started feeling older, and the warmth that a pair of sleeves provides was a welcome relief. Nowadays I will almost always pull them on before I touch the bar in the winter. And needless to say, I usually won't take a max without them, no matter how good my knees feel. They do provide a little bit of support, but I don't believe it is possible to get any carryover from knee sleeves. I like SBD knee sleeves. They have the most coverage, which is important to me because of my size, so they still give some warmth above and below the joint.

Knee Wraps

(*drumroll*)

Gear check

Here it is, *the* most controversial piece of equipment in raw powerlifting: Knee Wraps.

"But wait, wraps isn't raw. Wah, wah, wah..."

In all fairness, "raw" does mean "no bench shirt, no suit and no wraps." Lets not be divisive, though. Raw with wraps is still a type of raw. If powerlifting equipment was not so far removed from reality at this point there would not be any need for a "raw with wraps" division, but what do you want them to call it? How hard is it to say two words? "With wraps" or "without wraps," it is a pretty simple thing. I've never competed with knee wraps, but I don't get offended when people refer to knee wrap lifters as raw. I agree that it is important to distinguish between the two, but that is not hard to do. The vast majority of lifters I work with use knee wraps, so I am well versed in how much of a difference they can make.

Wraps dramatically effect the strength curve. When they are used correctly (that is something which takes a lot of skill and practice), they can provide a significant amount of assistance in what is typically the most difficult phase of the movement. This means a lifter who is trained to use them can have a much higher ceiling as far as squat numbers. When you train in them you are essentially training a special skill and overloading the least difficult phase of the lift. While that type of strength does not translate well into a "no wraps" squat (without additional training), it is absolutely necessary in the development of a competition wrapped squat. If you want to compete with wraps, you need to train with wraps for all of your working sets, at least.

It is worth mentioning that you should have a decent base of strength before you start training and competing in knee wraps and it is also a good idea to take some down time every so often and work on training your squat without wraps. It is imperative that you don't do this during your preparation for a wrapped

Gear check

competition, but immediately after a wrapped meet is a great time for a no wrapped cycle for a number of reasons.

If you know how to wrap, 2.5 meters is enough for almost anybody. You will have to try different types of wraps to find out what works best for you, but I recommend training in the same wraps you will use on the platform.

Chalk

Use chalk. Use it on your hands. Have someone apply it to your back to keep it dry, so the bar doesn't slip during squats or so you don't have trouble getting your traps to grip the bench. This should be a thoughtless thing. If the bar is loaded with heavy weight, put chalk on your hands before you touch it. Okay, good talk.

MSM lists for each lift

This list is not all-inclusive by any means. Feel free to get creative with these... within reason. Do not be the guy with accommodating resistance going both directions (reverse bands plus chains, etc.), or standing on bosu ball, or standing on anything for that matter, other than the floor, a block, or some mats. Think about your weak point in any given lift. Now think about which movement you can do with a barbell that would carry over the most into that weak point. You might not make the best choice, but anything you can justify with that train of logic is what I mean by "within reason." Below are some stalwart choices for the noted weak points.

MSM lists for each lift

For The Squat (Mid-Bar)

Front Squat

Weak point: quadriceps

- Start with the bar in the "front rack" position (haha, yeah right) or cross your arms over your shoulders with the bar over your clavicle and across the top of your deltoids. Keep the bar in this position throughout the lift.

- Keep your chest up, back and abdominal muscles tight, and your back flat.

- Fill your stomach with air and hold your breath the whole time the bar is in motion. You can stop and breathe at the top, between reps.

- This is a movement that will have good carryover into both your deadlift and your squat, so include these or SSB squats in your assistance work at least some of the time. Who doesn't want big quads? This is a no-brainer.

Safety Squat Bar

Weak point: upper back buckles; chest caves in; quadriceps

- Same rules as Front Squat, except you can just grab the handles for these.

Low Bar Squat

Weak point: hips, hamstrings or low back

- Grip the bar as narrow as your shoulders will allow, but not inside of elbows.

- Set the bar low on your traps across the top of the rear deltoids.

- Keep shoulder blades retracted and depressed (pinched together and pulled down).

MSM lists for each lift

- Take a wider than normal stance.
- Turn your chest up hard, overfill your lungs, and brace your core. Hold your breath throughout the movement.
- Squeeze the bar, but do not press into it or pull down on it at any point during the squat. Your upper back supports the bar not your arms.
- Keep your back flat as your hips move back and keep your knees out during the descent.
- Keep your chest up and drive your back into the bar as your drive your feet (mid-foot to heel) into the floor on the way up.

For The Bench Press

2 Board Press or Floor Press

Weak point: lockout

- Use the same set-up you would for a competition bench press.
- I prefer to take a narrow grip on these to really emphasize the triceps at lockout.
- Control your air while the bar is in motion.
- Lower the bar to the board, under control, and press. Do not smash the board.

Dead Press, from pins at the chest

Weak point: off of the chest

- Move a bench into the power rack and set the pins so that the bar will just touch your chest when you are set up on the bench.
- Get into position and set up under the loaded bar.

MSM lists for each lift

- Tighten back and abdominal muscles. Fill your lungs, and bear down. Then begin the press.
- Lower the weight to the pins under control.
- These are great for people who are slow coming off the chest, after the press command. Let's face it, everyone can benefit from being stronger and faster off the chest. This lift is best performed for sets of 3 as an assistance MSM in a meet prep cycle.

1" Pause Press

Weak point: acceleration off of chest

- Again, use competition bench press set up.
- Lower the bar and stop it 1" from chest.
- Pause for a two count.
- Press the bar back up to lockout.

For The Deadlift (Conventional)

Rack Pulls, below the knees

Weak point: lockout

- Set the pins so that the bar sits below your knees at the start of the lift.
- Lean back and drive your heel and center of foot into the floor.
- Drive your hips forward into the bar.
- Be certain you are starting in the same position you would be in at this point in the lift if you had pulled from the floor. This is crucial for carryover. Film yourself pulling from both starting points, compare, and correct if

MSM lists for each lift

you have to. This can also be done for mat or block pulls.

- These can serve you well as an MSM for hypertrophy. Also. For that purpose, sets sets of 8-10 reps are best.
- Always reset every rep, never bounce off the rack.

2-3" Deficit Deadlift

Weak point: start of lift

- Greater than 3" deficit is not a good idea.
- Less than 2" deficit is not sufficient variance for the desired effect.
- Start the lift with a straight back, keep it that way.
- Focus on keeping your hips lower than your shoulders throughout the movement.
- Keep the bar close to you.
- Drive your hips forward when the bar reaches your knees.

2-3" Mat or Block Pulls

Weak point: acceleration off of the floor

- Get everything extremely tight at the start of this lift. (arms, back, abs, legs)
- Keep everything tight throughout.
- Again, low back straight, keep it straight.
- Once you are set up and tight, initiate this lift by pulling the slack out of the bar with straight arms and then, in an explosive manner, try to accelerate.

- Be certain you are starting in the same position you would be in at this point in the lift if you had pulled from the floor. This is crucial for carryover. Film yourself pulling from both starting points, compare and correct if you have to. This can also be done for rack pulls.

Preferred Assistance Exercises

Chins/Pull ups

Chins are and always have been a staple in my training. I don't think I've done a training cycle in the last ten year that didn't involve chins in one form or another. Certain templates will have you adding weight for these, while others will have you going for max reps. Both are very effective ways to train this exercise.

Whether supinated, pronated, or neutral grip, I like to do chins with with my upper back arched in extension and my chest pushed out. I imagine I am bringing the bar down during a bench press as I pull my chest up in the direction of the bar. I feel like I get a lot more carryover into stability on the bench press when I do my back exercises this way, thinking about the bar path for my bench.

It's also worth mentioning that about 90% of my bicep work is done in the form of chins. They work.

Barbell Rows

I developed an extremely thick back during the years I competed in bodybuilding, using a combination of rows, but this has always been the king of them. Just like chins, barbell rows are an indispensable exercise when it comes to developing the musculature of the mid and upper back. When you do these correctly they have great carryover into stability and control of bar placement for bench press, not to mention deadlift or squat which benefit from a thick, strong back for more obvious reasons.

Barbell rows should be at the very forefront of assistance exercise selection for overall back size and strength. After bracing and taking the bar from the rack, start in a standing position with your back arched and bring your hip back as you tilt your torso forward. I like to go a little further than 45 degrees with my torso and let my arms hang forward at the bottom of the lift, rowing my elbows back so the bar touches on my stomach. I'm always thinking about the eccentric portion of my bench press during these and every kind of row. I recommend a focused, controlled eccentric for barbell rows, slightly slower than the concentric.

Barbell Shrugs

I see a lot of people doing barbell shrugs like they are a competitive lift. The last time I checked, there was no "shrug" division in powerlifting. I've even seen people attempting to do "shrugs" with more weight than they can deadlift. That is just batshit crazy, I will leave it there.

I personally think these are a great assistance exercise and, when they are employed correctly, they're great for hypertrophy. Please don't overlook that clause: "when they are employed correctly." Barbell shrugs should be performed with a full range of motion. I like these done with the chin down, which lengthens what is otherwise an extremely short range of motion. Come all the way up so your shoulders are raising behind your head in a straight line from the bottom of the movement. No shrugging back, or up and back or any of that; up and down. I recommend a cadence of one up, two down, really slowing things down at the top.

Preferred Assistance Exercises

Chest Supported Dumbbell Rows

After my spine surgery I fell in love with this movement, maybe out of necessity. For the first time in my life I was unable to perform barbell rows (for a few months), due to the nature of the procedures I had done. I needed to find a way to maintain my back development and after playing around with a few other options I knew these were it.

Set up an incline bench at 45 degrees or as close to that as you can. Straddle the bench and lay on it, stomach down with your feet on the floor. You want to keep your whole spine in extension as you perform these, so brace your torso and arch your whole back. Take a dumbbell in each hand with a somewhat neutral grip and row them up. You wont be able to handle weights as heavy as you would with a barbell row, but you are loading each arm, independently, and I have never felt my lats or the muscles of my mid back work like they do on this exercise. Again, I think about bringing the bar down on a bench press as I row the dumbbells up.

Chest Supported Dumbbell Shrugs

This is a great assistance exercise for lifters who have trouble keeping their shoulders back during the bench press. Your traps and rhomboids are going to improve from these if you do them correctly. Set up for these exactly the same way you set up for chest supported dumbbell rows: stomach down on the bench at 45 degrees, back arched and torso braced. With one dumbbell in each hand and your arms straight, shrug the dumbbells up in a vertical line from where they hang in your hands. Use a one up, two down cadence for these. This is a movement you are going to want to do for higher reps most of the time.

Two Board Press

The raw powerlifting community tends to go one of two ways when it comes to board presses. Either lifter's treat them like they are as useful of a tool for raw strength as they are for shirted bench work, or they scoff at the idea of doing board presses of any kind, because "that stuff is only for geared lifters." As usual, I find myself somewhere in between. I think a 2 board press is a useful assistance exercise and a great way to improve lockout strength. For the purpose of this program, they fit into the category of an MSM. I've only included them in this section to point out the fact that a raw lifter should never post a video of a 2 board "PR" on social media. Even if you use the conjugate method, which is a great system, no one cares how much you can 2 board press. Seriously, it's tantamount to a barbell shrug PR. Just keep that to yourself.

Preferred Assistance Exercises

Wide Grip Bench Press

These will typically be used as a main movement on your second pressing day. Nothing will inflate your pecs quite like these do. Even my lats are pumped when I finish these. In fact, be prepared for your whole upper body to be painfully swollen after a couple of sets of these for 25 reps.

Take a grip two fingers wider than your competition grip, if that is possible, the only exception being that you do not go wider than legal grip, which is "index finger on the ring." Use a hand off for these if you are doing the very high rep protocol, and as soon as you are locked in, start moving the bar as quickly as possible. Continue until you either get twenty five reps or are unable to complete another rep. Use a spotter to help you get back in the rack, because after this many reps nothing works the way it's supposed to and it's easy to make an avoidable mistake that could get you hurt.

Incline Dumbbell Press

This is another exercise which is a good selection for the main movement on your second pressing day. One major benefit of incline dumbbell presses is that you can take a neutral grip, which can be a lot easier on beat up shoulders, while still allowing you to stimulate hypertrophy in all of the pressing muscles. If you are using a template which has these set at the very high rep protocol, you'll be doing at least 30 reps, which

Preferred Assistance Exercises

becomes something like a religious experience as the weights get heavy.

Rolling Tricep Extension

These hit the triceps and lats pretty effectively, so it is no surprise that they are one of my favorite assistance exercises for bench press. I recommend moving up in reps over a period of a few microcycles and then moving the weight up and starting with a lower number of reps, then repeating. In my experience, progressing in this manner has helped avoid inflammation and elbow pain.

Preferred Assistance Exercises

Seated Military Press

I can sum up all I have to say about overhead work in this paragraph. Pressing overhead is a great way to build powerful shoulders and triceps. Do you need to do an overhead pressing movement in your training to excel in powerlifting? No.

The answer is no; unequivocally, no. They are as dispensable as any other assistance exercise. For some powerlifters, overhead pressing movements can be a problem. When I say they can be a problem, I mean they can irritate the shoulder and cause pain that can interfere with the lifters ability to perform the competitive movements. (Before you rush to the defense of the overhead, ask yourself: if I were recommending that someone experiencing acute pain from barbell rows should stop doing them, if you'd be as zealous to defend those.)

Using dumbbells instead of a bar and taking a neutral grip or using a swiss bar that allows neutral grip for overhead will minimize the pain and irritation in most lifters who have trouble, but some problems don't need to be solved, only acknowledged and avoided.

A large number of powerlifters do great with these and find them to be an awesome assistance exercise for bench press. By all means, consult a medical professional if you think there is a shoulder injury which is causing pain when you try to press overhead, but bear in mind: you do not have to press overhead.

You can argue with me about this until you are blue in the face, but the fact remains: you do not have to press overhead in powerlifting. I built a 550 pound raw bench press never having done a single overhead pressing movement in more than 8 years. I've coached lifters who have put up top ranking numbers in all of the lifts without ever pressing overhead.

Everything I said in the last paragraph notwithstanding, I think a strict seated military press, if it doesn't cause issues, is the better

Preferred Assistance Exercises

choice for assistance for a powerlifter, since the goal will be mainly hypertrophy, and you aren't training a competitive overhead press. I've started doing these again within the last year and, on a side note, they don't seem to bother my shoulder as much in the bottom position as a standing overhead press does, for whatever reason.

Standing Overhead Press

Most lifters do well with a relatively narrow grip on these, somewhere around shoulder width. I personally prefer to lock my thumbs around the bar, but many lifters I have worked with have done better with a thumbless, false grip or "suicide grip," citing that it helps them keep the bar close. Be certain not to drop the bar on your face if you choose that type of grip: you don't want it *that* close.

Dips

Dips are another really great exercise for building big strong triceps, pecs and shoulders. These work great with weight added, as a main movement on your second pressing day for sets of 25; or for sets of 8-15, you can work them in as a bench press assistance exercise; or you can choose to never do them at all. This is another one that some people have weird stabbing shoulder pain with. My general rule is if something hurts like that, don't do it, especially if it is not something you *must* do.

Side Raise

Side laterals, side raises, whatever you want to call these, you can do them with both arms at once or one arm at a time, however you prefer. Play around with them and see what works best for you. It doesn't matter too much how you do them, because they aren't a very important exercise. When I was

Preferred Assistance Exercises

younger I would do them really heavy, but over time I realized that I was able to hit the deltoids more effectively doing higher reps, maybe 20, with a moderate weight.

Rear Raise

The same goes for these as for side raises. A higher rep range seems to work better. I seem to be able to isolate the posterior deltoid better doing one arm at a time, but if I'm in a hurry I will do both sides at once, because, again, it doesn't really matter. If you don't allow the dumbbells to come all of the way down, you can keep constant tension on the muscle and that is a good thing for hypertrophy.

Cable Tricep Extension

There is not an huge amount to say about these. They are a tricep extension, performed using a cable machine. You can use a single arm handle or a bar. They are a great way to finish off your triceps and are probably best performed one arm at a time, although that is not crucial. I prefer to start with an underhand extension first when I do these and then move on to an overhand extension. This is one exercise where I will always keep the reps high.

Hammer Curls

These are best performed across the chest and at the end of a training session that involved chins.

Preferred Assistance Exercises

Band Pull-Apart

There is definitely more than one way to do these. Grab a band and pull it apart, there is really no wrong way to do that. I prefer them done as shown below: on a band which is choked around the top of a power rack with each hand grasping one side of the two straps of band hanging from above.

I start with my thumbs pointing down when I grab the band, then I turn my hands out and pull apart until the bottom of the band touches my chest. It's probably a good idea to do a minimum of 30 reps per set for these, 3-5 sets.

Preferred Assistance Exercises

Reverse Hyper Machine

It is possible that I am the world's biggest fan of the reverse hyper machine, invented by Louie Simmons. This thing helped me build a back that I used to say was indestructible. Of course when I opened Keyhole Barbell I had to get by with the bare minimum for a few years. So, I didn't buy one at first. I tell people all the time I do not believe I would have ended up needing emergency spine surgery if I had bought one and kept up my normal regimen when I moved out here. I ended up buying one immediately after the surgery and it was a huge part of my rehab. I prefer to use a strap for these and I train them twice per microcycle. One day I do a heavy weight for sets of 10 and the other I use a light weight for sets of 15-20. I always do 5 sets of these.

Pull Through

These can be done with a low cable machine or a band. I've seen them done with both at once, but I'm not going to go as far as saying that will benefit you in any way that one or the other wouldn't. I recommend 15-20 reps for these. I'm not going to give you a hard number of sets which must be done, but I will say you should keep it at or below 5. No more than 5 sets is a good general rule for all assistance exercises, anyway.

Preferred Assistance Exercises

Leg Curl

This is another exercise that I have seen yield better results with a slower eccentric portion of the rep. These can be done one leg at a time, or you can do both at once. I recommend the 8-15 rep range for these, but definitely not any higher. I have experimented with higher reps and the results were not desirable, across the board.

Calf Raises

Do these. Just do them. Take the time and do some boring ass calf work at least one day per microcycle. I realize it is hard to get excited about these and it is very possible to get by without them, but if you are doing a bicep isolation exercise and no direct

Preferred Assistance Exercises

calf work, you are headed the way of the douche. 5 sets of 8-10 reps is fine, but if you want to do a higher or lower rep range, that works, too. If you want to include them on a second day, that is also not a bad idea. A good way to set that up is to do them on squat and deadlift days, after your main lift and MSM, or at the end of the session.

The Elephant In The Room

Performance Enhancing Drugs and Powerlifting

Every effective thing has a cost equal to it's efficacy. This is true for everything in life, and I've found that in some cases the cost is even greater than the efficacy.

Something which increases strength both dramatically and quickly, does so at a cost and, quite frankly, that cost will prevent you from doing it for very long. This is true when it comes to training methodologies and implements, as well as massive doses of performance enhancing drugs.

Just because it's possible to recover from an insane amount of work while using high doses of these drugs does not mean it's necessary to do that amount of work or even beneficial. You also have to consider that no matter what amount of drugs you pump into your body there is still a point of diminished return and it is still very possible to overtrain and more than likely, if you are doing as much work as possible while on these drugs, you will not be able to intelligently scale back that workload enough to allow you to continue to train and recover when you stop taking drugs. Enter, the guy or girl who never comes off of drugs. (At least not until they are forced to, at which point they stop lifting.)

I will tell you unequivocally, regardless of what you hear on the internet, that for the most part the strongest people in the world are not, in fact, using crazy amounts of steroids, at least not for the vast majority of their training. Some do, both male and female, and it seems to me that these are the only ones who are willing to discuss PED publicly at all, which provides a very one-sided picture, giving outsiders and beginners the impression that this is what everyone does. That is just not the case. The only thing that pretty much every top lifter has in common is training consistently for many years and a decent "hand me down" from mom and dad.

The takeaway

You can use just about any intelligent, systemized training program (if you've invested the time and money to have someone who knows teach you the basics of proper technique) and based on what I've seen, over a period of many years, you can get very close to the level you would if you worked with a high level coach every step of the way and perfected the minutia with charts, graphs, stopwatches and all of the other contrived bullshit. It will just take you a little longer. The same goes for not using steroids (or at least waiting to use them and there is a good argument for that).

If you suck at something, steroids aren't going to change that. I find it funny that so many new lifters go on and on about what kind of steroids they plan to take, these elaborate, expensive courses of drugs, but when it comes to hiring someone to, you know, actually teach them how to fucking lift, they can't afford anything like that.

Why, you might ask, are some lifters able to get to an elite, world class competitive level of strength (let's call them "Group A"), while others flounder for many years ("Group B") to reach the level where the first group started? Clearly, Group A is on steroids and Group B is all natural, right? The answer is simple, but not *that* simple. In all honesty, it is likely that some lifters from each group are using PED. The difference is that lifters in the Group A possess a genetically inherited capacity for strength and dexterity in performing the lifts and perhaps an amount of discipline which Group B simply does not. The ceiling of potential for Group A is logically going to be much higher than that of Group B. And I'm sorry to break your heart, princess, but with or without steroids, the vast majority of lifters are in Group B.

The Elephant In The Room

What nobody wants to hear when starting a new program is that it is going to take years to make serious progress. You only need to open any muscle magazine to see what people want to read. Maximum results, minimal effort and a program that will make you strong and jacked in six weeks.

Well, I'm here to give you what you need, not what you want.

If you haven't been training with a systemized program and competing for at least a few years and you're already talking about drugs, you need to rethink your priorities. It is easy to make progress in the beginning. Take advantage of that. Eat a lot of food. Get enough rest. Stick to a program long enough for it to work. These are the things you should be focusing on, not obsessing about steroids. As I mentioned earlier, the fact that a lot of you wont spend the money to hire a coach to help with your technique, but are in a big hurry to spend your last dime on steroids or worthless supplements is absurd.

Whether or not you decide to take drugs is a personal decision, but you should know first, it's going to take years either way. That's right, even if you have the genetics and talent of Eric Spoto (who benched 620lb raw before ever using drugs, by the way) and you decide to jump on some gear your first year lifting, it's still going to take you 15 or more years to get where he is, if you ever do. And you probably won't last the distance from here to there if you go that route. What I mean is that if you start using early in your training, you more than likely will never learn how to train without steroids and your success in lifting will be entirely dependent on drugs, making you no better than a run of the mill drug addict who needs them to get by, or in this case, to even be strong at all.

So now, the question everyone side-steps about their programs.

The Elephant In The Room
Is this a program designed for lifters who take steroids?

To answer that completely, I have to first provide a little back story. I've been a trainer/coach and writing programs for sixteen years. The first incarnation of the 5thSet program came about around ten years ago, because I found myself in a place with very limited training resources, sub-par nutrition and absolutely no access to any type of PED or even protein supplements: State Prison.

I had a training group which consisted of myself and at least four or five other experienced guys, at any given time, who consistently followed my programs. It was all but impossible to test a 1RM, except for maybe one day per month when we would have access to the inside gym and I would only have them test the max for one lift at that time. As a result a max for each lift could only be taken every three months.

We would usually have to train outside with very limited weights so this meant the percentages had to be dialed back. I used the Prilepin Table to estimate the amount of volume that would be required and eventually developed a novel way to self regulate, which would also help with hypertrophy.

I was never really able to squat or deadlift with much more than 70% of my 1RM, due to lack of available weight in the yard. Nevertheless, I was able to get very close to the level of strength I was at prior to being incarcerated, training in this manner. The lifters I worked with also got very strong, without good nutrition or drugs. This time in my life was a lesson on many levels, but in regard to training it taught me how little you really need to make progress if the program is scalable and systemized.

I've had ten years or so to experiment and improve on the program, so the percentages and total work have changed slightly, but the framework is very much the same. I've tried

The Elephant In The Room

changing the number of sets and some other key points, but nothing has worked as well, so time and again I've come back to the original set-up. I don't believe there is a more effective way, on the long term, to train for strength than this.

So, the short answer is: no, it was not designed for lifters who take steroids. It was designed for a group of lifters who didn't have the option of taking steroids.

That is not to say that it is not the best program for lifters who do use PED, because I strongly believe it is. It allows lifters who have been using to make consistent progress even when they are already at a high level as well as (and this is huge) maintain their level of strength to a great degree while taking time "off" of steroids completely or using a low, TRT type dose for part of the year, either of which will lengthen the amount of time someone is able to continue making progress. During these phases, it is advisable to avoid testing 1RM for intermediate to advanced lifters. I've seen better results just rolling back to the initial percentage the next microcycle, after deloading when they "fail-out". Remember that progress is not always linear. This is a marathon and not a sprint. No one gets to the top overnight.

5thSet works great for natural lifters, also, because it is self-regulating and provides a very rigid structure that prevents you from doing too much and burning out, but at the same time ensures enough work is being performed at the appropriate percentages to consistently hit PRs. The system was developed and tested working with drug-free lifters, after all.

It is a versatile and scalable program which I have successfully adapted for everyone from newbie CrossFitters who want to try their hand at barbell club, to both male and female powerlifters competing at the very highest level of the sport.

The Elephant In The Room
A brief word about PED use in females and how it effects this program

As I have repeatedly stated, the decision to use or not use drugs is a personal one. That decision should be made with all of the potential physical and legal consequences in mind. I'll start by saying that it's possible for a female to make it to the top level in powerlifting without drug use of any kind. I have seen it with my own eyes. I've been a coach long enough to know that athletes will do what they will do in this department regardless of my opinion. And while I will give my opinion to the people I work with, I always make it clear that I am here to help, either way. I've had athletes lie to me about drug use in the past which makes my job next to impossible, so I like to encourage dialogue and I let it be known that I will generally provide advice without judgement on the subject. With that said, regarding women who choose to use performance enhancing drugs:

Much the same as I would recommend for drug free men, I encourage women who use to chase PRs, still do the meet peaking cycle and test 1RM when they are scheduled to do so on this program, even when they are "off" for the simple fact that when they are "on" they are not dramatically above their normal recoverability, due to the micro dosing necessary to avoid androgynous side effects. This program, for a woman who uses, runs the same whether she is on PED or not, whereas men who cycle on and off should just run the program and do the deloads without ever trying to peak or test 1RM while "off."

As far as women who disregard concern for androgynous side effects and use dosing and hormones similar to what a man would use: refer back to the first two paragraphs of this chapter. It won't last long and if it does, they won't be women. That's as far as I will get into it, because **women do not need that much, if anything, to compete and win at the highest level** when they have the potential to do so. If someone doesn't have the potential to start with, no amount of milligrams will ever make up for that.

For women, PED should be less about an immediate performance enhancement and more about recovery enhancement. As a woman it is your own responsibility to understand exactly what and how much you are taking as well as who you are taking advice from. What you put into your body can change the way you look and sound for the rest of your life. If you are truly confused about the safest options a female has, there is help out there and there are people who have a wealth of experience with these things. (Not your boyfriend.)

If you make the conscious choice to continue down a path which is giving you appreciable side effects; the choice to go the way of the gender hybrid, don't pretend it's because you are "hardcore" or "willing to do what others won't" or anything noble like that. That talk encourages women to do it, who might not otherwise.

That "sacrifice" is more likely about an underlying psychological condition than a desire to win, if you're saying that you are willing to become a man to get there. Be honest with yourself.

Again, it's a personal choice, but if glory is what you are looking for, keep in mind that no one is impressed by a balding woman with a five o'clock shadow, who cant remember the last time she had a period, lifting weights that pretty much *any* guy can lift. Take a minute and think about that.

Everyone who sees it is thinking it. If more people talked about it, openly, maybe less girls would do this to themselves. If you have what it takes to do well in this sport, you can do it without destroying yourself. The last thing I want to do is hurt any woman's feelings, but these are things that need to be said and what we currently have is a shame driven lack of dialogue which isn't helping anyone.

Frequently Asked Questions

Do you ever have people run other programs?

I would never let my ego as a coach prevent the success of a lifter. I will not hesitate to use another program that I feel is better for a certain application than one of my own and I have done it in certain circumstances. I have experimented in my own training over the last decade or so with hybrid versions of this program from time to time, when I was bored, always looking to find a way to improve things. I've even run a 5thSet/Conjugate hybrid template for a couple of mesocycles with some success. For one reason or another, nothing ever seems to work out as well, or for as long, as the "real deal" with the rules I've laid out in this book. Something mixed is something weakened, as they say. It's worth mentioning that I have people I've worked with for years with great success that have only ever used 5thSet. If it's not broken, don't fix it.

Tarra Oravec totaled 830 at her first meet and at that point the only program she had ever run was 5thSet. She won Champion of Champions at RUM this year, then totaled 1135 at the Women's Pro/Am, and that does not include the easiest 485lb deadlift I've ever seen in my life, which she pulled on a fourth attempt. She did 8 meets in 2 years and PR'd her total at every single one and the only program she has ever used is 5thSet. She has continued to make regular progress on this program for over 3 years and she is not an outlier in that regard.

Should I do any cardio? How much?

The role of cardiovascular training for the powerlifter is an aid to recovery and overall health as there is very little need for an increase in cardiovascular capacity to perform in competition. There is an argument that cardio can help with training endurance and recovery between sets, but 3 x 40 minute, low-moderate intensity sessions per week is sufficient for this effect.

This program is designed to leave enough recovery in the bucket for the average person to do just about that amount. My usual rule is no more than 9 miles per week on foot, spread over 3 sessions, and you can decide if you want to run, walk or crawl it.

Can back work be done on bench days?

Yes. In fact I have had some success doing the chins on my bench day, after a bench MSM, with very little other assistance work. I've even done some of the chins between my lighter warm up sets for bench. The main thing to consider is the way it effects the rest of your cycle.

When I do them on my bench day, I make sure to split up the assistance work (rows) from the main work on the following session and do it the day after that session, so I'm not training back two sessions in a row.

Is it ever okay to skip a scheduled training day? If so, when?

Is it ever okay? Yes. However this is not something you want to make a habit of for obvious reasons. There is enough leeway to get away with this maybe 1-2 times per mesocycle and I'd rather have you do that than fail out on your 5thSet because you worked late; or you are sick, or you're hung over from a birthday party or whatever aspect of the real world showed up and pissed all over your dreams of greatness.

Frequently Asked Questions

One of the most beautiful aspects of the 9 day cycle is that it can effortlessly become the 11 day cycle, if the need arises, and that will have little or no impact on the outcome so long as it doesn't become a habit. Pick up where you left off on the next scheduled day. Never skip a session, do the scheduled session next time you train.

When is it okay? I have rule for this I share with my lifters. Ask yourself: "Will I suck?" Whatever the reason you are considering skipping a scheduled training day: "Will I suck?" If you're pretty sure it's a yes and you're going to fail out or perform poorly because you didn't recover due to real world circumstances: instead of the weight room, hit the bedroom. Get another light cardio session in that week or just take it easy. Rest and destroy.

When is it not okay? The meet peaking phase comes to mind. If you are beat up going into your max microcycle in the beginning of the meet peaking mesocycle, skip a scheduled day before you start. After that you really want to avoid missing anything until after the 80% week.

Can the second pressing day be used as a "dynamic effort" day or a speed day?

Yes. It can be and the program works just as well that way. I have had people do this in preparation for a meet during the meet peaking phase with about the same results as the very high rep protocol.

This is a good option year round for a lifter who doesn't necessarily need to add much muscle, but would benefit from technical improvement in the bench press.

The proper protocol to use the second pressing day as a speed day is to make the main movement a competition grip bench press and perform 5 sets of 3 reps starting with 60% of 1RM for

Frequently Asked Questions

the first microcycle, with the emphasis being on speed and technical perfection. You have the option of adding 5 pounds per microcycle, or you can keep the weight at 60%.

Can the second pressing day be used for an overhead pressing day?

Yep. We have played with this option, too. If you are going to use the very high rep protocol, you will do better with dumbbells for overhead.

If you want to train it like a lighter strength training movement, you'll probably use a barbell and start with 3 sets of 5 reps at 60% 1RM. Either option works well.

Is it ever okay to do a mesocycle of box squats?

There are times when it is definitely not a bad idea.

A good example would be a lifter who competes with wraps, coming off of a meet, who is due for a no wraps mesocycle. In this instance I will usually have the lifter use box squats for the first no wraps mesocycle, because they break the eccentric-concentric chain, which is favorable for building strength in what is by far the most underdeveloped phase of the movement for a wrapped squatter. I will lose the box on the second or third mesocycle for this application.

Box squats can also just be used as a stimulus variable here and there for a microcycle or two, as long as you aren't close to a meet.

Lastly, they are suitable to use as an MSM.

Frequently Asked Questions

I have an MSM that I started at 70% of my technique/speed lift last microcycle. I am about to start a new microcycle and reset my technique/speed lift to 70%. Do I have to reset the MSM, or should I roll into a new cycle and keep adding 5 pounds per week?

You can reset the MSM each cycle or you can just knock some weight off and meet yourself half way, providing a little extra intensity to a weak point. The deciding factor is usually the lift selection. For example, if your technique/speed lift is deadlift and your MSM selection is a deficit deadlift, that's an example of a time you might want to reset to 70% every cycle. Front squat as an MSM for a technique/speed squat is another good example. However, this is not a rule. You can play with it, that's what I do: adjust for the individual needs of the lifter.

How much pain is normal? How do I know the difference between the type of pain I can "train through" and a legitimate injury?

I have a question I have my lifters ask themselves for this one, too.

"Is it preventing me from using the muscle or joint normally in the execution of a lift?"

If the answer is yes, you have an injury and it should be treated as such. That is to say you should see a doctor.

Shoulder pain, elbow pain or anything else which is transient and likely being caused by inflammation or overuse can usually be mitigated by backing off of the movement or movements suspected to instigate symptoms. I have found various recovery modalities to be useful, such as flossing joints using a compression wrap, though I will not make any recommendations on that subject.

Can I do a mesocycle with a specialty bar for one of the main lifts? If so, when?

Absolutely. You could do it for bench press with a buffalo bar. You could use a safety squat bar or even the buffalo bar for squat. This is not something you will want to do frequently, however, and never too close to a meet,

I have used a buffalo bar while running speed bench on the 2nd pressing day, also. The idea was to provide a stimulus variable; though, at the expense of technical improvement.

It's important to understand that you do not need to use specialty bars in your training to improve as a lifter. They can be a useful tool or an obstacle when misapplied. If you don't understand why you are doing something, you probably should not do it.

How much fatigue is normal?

This is a very difficult question, because the answer is going to vary, depending on the specific goal, the current phase of training and the lifter. The first few microcycles of a meet peaking cycle, you will accumulate a tremendous amount of fatigue. This will also be true during some other stages of your training, like the fourth and fifth microcycle of any mesocycle.

I would say experiencing little or no signs of fatigue at any point mid-way through a mesocycle or greater would be abnormal. This is a sign that too much recovery has been left "on the table," so to speak.

On the other hand the human body is capable of only a finite amount of recovery and physiological adaptation in a given period of time. To understand that is to know that overload is something which should be applied progressively, over a number of weeks and not overnight. So, you might be running into trouble if you are devastated at the beginning of your second microcycle on this program, having only really trained four times. Keep in mind that things usually even out during the second mesocycle on this program, fatigue-wise.

How can I help recovery?

The biggest limiting factor for a lifter is their own inherent natural level of recoverability and adaptability. Everyone has the general ability to recover and adapt, but for various reasons, some people are more inclined to excel in this department than most. There is nothing you can do to make yourself one of those people if you are not already.

What you can do is maximize your body's ability to recover by getting proper nutrition, and enough rest.

Eight hours is enough sleep for an athlete and it's not exactly an impossible task. This is another thing people look at me like I am crazy when I tell them. They know they would benefit from eight hours of sleep per night, but will claim it is impossible for them.

Like anything else you know you should do: if you don't do it, it's not that important to you.

Most people will ask questions they already know the answer to and hope you will give another answer. Like you were probably hoping to read: "Get a massage," or something like that. Okay, get a massage, but you still need to get enough sleep.

The nutrition aspect of this is not terribly complicated. Eat enough calories and protein to recover from training. If you are somewhat active, fifteen calories per pound of body weight is a good starting point to figure out your maintenance calories. One gram of protein per pound of body weight is a good rule of thumb to figure out your protein requirements. The amount of carbohydrates you need is going to vary, depending on your level of physical activity. You can try to play with these things yourself or hire someone to help you, but do not disregard nutrition and then complain about not being able to recover or improve. This is one of the few things you have control over.

There are very few things you can do to actually improve your recovery: rest and nutrition are the two most important factors. I would not be answering this question completely if I did not mention that performance enhancing drugs can dramatically improve recovery and, for this reason, a lot of powerlifters use them. Even with drugs, however, it is impossible to improve without adequate nutrition and rest

The Templates

Please keep the rules in mind when using these templates. As I outlined in the "Progressions" section, any lift that calls for 80% (5thSet Protocol) should first be performed, for a full mesocycle, starting with 77.5%. The Technique/Speed lifts should be reset to 70% at the beginning of each mesocycle. It is alright to reduce the amount of assistance work on a template, but not to increase it. Stick to whatever you decide for a full mesocycle at minimum.

The Templates

Deadlift- Technique/Speed Template, Assistance Variant #1

(wide grip rep bench, floor press, barbell rows, high rep chins)

Bench (1):

- Flat Bench Press (Competition Grip): 80% 1RM (77.5% first mesocycle), 4 sets of 2 repetitions, followed by 5th set of AMRAP.

  ***Add 5 pounds to the bar per cycle for 5 microcycles or until you are only able to perform 3 reps on the 5thSet, which ever comes FIRST. At this point deload all training for one microcycle. Start over with 80% and go for rep PRs on 5thSets whenever possible.

- Floor Press (1/2 of a thumb from the smooth): 2 sets of 15 reps, first set: use 45% 1RM, second set: start with same weight. Hold the first set and add 5 lbs to the second set the following week, every time you get all of your target reps.

- Side Raises: 2 progressive sets of 10 reps, start sub-max and move up each week until you are near a 10RM, then maintain the weight as this will become static volume. Try to slow down the negative portion of each rep.

- Rear Raises: Same directions and volume as Side Raises, except you will shoot for 12 reps and focus on maintaining tension, not allowing the dumbbells to come all of the way down.

Squat (2):

- Squat: 80% 1RM for 4 sets of 2 reps followed by 5th set of AMRAP. Move up 5 per cycle, same rules as bench.
- Reverse Hyper: 5 sets of 10 reps.
- Barbell Rows (overhand): 2 progressive sets of 12 reps, start with medium weight and add to the second set the following cycle whenever target(12) reps are achieved.
- Heavy dumbbell rows to lower chest: 1 set of 15 reps, move up next cycle whenever target reps are achieved.
- Heavy Barbell Shrugs: 2 progressive sets of 15, same rules.
- Calf Raises: 5 sets of 10 reps.

Bench (3):

- Wide Grip Bench (2 fingers wider than comp): 52.5% for 2 sets of 25 reps. When you get 25 on both sets, move up 5 lbs the following cycle.
- Rolling Tricep Ext: 2 progressive sets of 12-20 reps. First set should be very easy. Do 12 reps the first cycle, the next cycle 15 reps, next 18, next 20, next: +5lbs x 12 reps, repeat.
- Cable Tricep Ext: 2 sets of 25 reps each arm, overhand; followed by 2 sets of 25 reps each arm, underhand. Use the same weight on all 4 sets. When you get 25 reps on all sets for 2 weeks, move up 5 pounds.
- Band Pull Aparts: 3 sets of 30-35 reps, 60 seconds rest between sets. Move down to 45 seconds rest after 2 weeks, then up the reps to 35 with 60 seconds, then 35 reps with 45 seconds, then add a 4th set and follow that pattern. Do not go above 5 sets.

Deadlift (4):

- Deadlift (Competition): 70% 1RM, 5 sets of 3 repetitions, add 5 pounds per microcycle. The emphasis is going to be on technique and speed off the floor.
- Rack Pulls(below knee): 70% 1RM, 3 sets of 3 reps.
- Rev Hyper or Pull Throughs: 3 sets of 15 reps.
- Chins: Warm up first with 2 sets of light pulldowns. If you don't have a pull down machine, use a band to warm up by choking it around the top of a squat rack and doing pull downs on your knees. Start with body weight- 1 set for max reps, pronated. 1 set for max reps, supinated. When you can get 20 reps on both sets add a chain the following microcycle or use a belt to load weight. (If you cant do at least 5 chins, pick the template with chins for high sets.) No neutral grip on these for this template. If you get shoulder pain when pronated (overhand), do both sets supinated.
- Hammer Curls: 2 progressive sets of 12-15 reps.

The Templates

Deadlift- Technique/Speed Template, Assistance Variant #2

(incline dumbbell rep bench, board press, dumbbell rows, high set chins)

Bench (1):

- Flat Bench Press (Competition Grip): 80% 1RM (77.5% first mesocycle), 4 sets of 2 repetitions, followed by 5th set of AMRAP.

  ***Add 5 pounds to the bar per cycle for 5 microcycles or until you are only able to perform 3 reps on the 5thSet, which ever comes FIRST. At this point deload all training for one microcycle. Start over with 80% and go for rep PRs on 5thSets whenever possible.

- 2 board press (1/2 of a thumb from the smooth): 2 sets of 15 reps, first set use 45% of full ROM 1RM, second set start with same weight. Hold the first set and add 5 lbs to the second set the following cycle, every time you get all of your target reps.

- Side Raises: 2 progressive sets of 10 reps, start sub-max and move up each cycle until you are near a 10RM, then maintain the weight as this will become static volume. Try to slow down the negative portion of each rep.

- Rear Raises: Same directions and volume as Side Raises, except you will shoot for 12 reps and focus on maintaining tension, not allowing the dumbbells to come all of the way down.

Squat (2):

- Squat: 80% 1RM for 4 sets of 2 reps followed by 5th set of AMRAP. Move up 5 per cycle, same rules as bench.
- Reverse Hyper: 5 sets of 10 reps.
- Dumbbell Rows, chest supported on incline bench (both hands): 3 sets of 20 reps, start with a medium intensity weight and add to the second set the following cycle whenever target (20) reps are achieved.
- Dumbbell Shrugs, chest supported on incline bench: 3 sets of 20 reps, same rules.
- Calf Raises: 5 sets of 10 reps.

Bench (3):

- Incline Dumbbell Press (45 degree bench, neutral grip): medium weight for 30 reps. When you get 30 on both sets, move up 5 lbs the following cycle.
- Rolling Tricep Ext: 2 progressive sets of 12-20 reps. First set should be very easy. The first cycle do 12 reps, the next cycle 15 reps, next 18, next 20, next: +5lbs x 12 reps, repeat.
- Cable Tricep Ext: 2 sets of 25 reps each arm, overhand; followed by 2 sets of 25 reps each arm, underhand. Use the same weight on all 4 set, if you get 25 reps on all sets for 2 cycles, move up 5 pounds.
- Band Pull Aparts: 3 sets of 30-35 reps, 60 seconds rest between sets. Move down to 45 seconds rest after 2 cycles, then up the reps to 35 with 60 seconds, then 35 reps with 45 seconds, then add a 4th set and follow that pattern. Do not go above 5 sets.

Deadlift (4):

- Deadlift (Competition): 70% 1RM, 5 sets of 3 repetitions, add 5 pounds per microcycle. The emphasis is going to be on technique and speed off the floor.
- Rack Pulls(below knee): 70% 1RM, 3 sets of 3 reps.
- Rev Hyper or Pull Throughs: 3 sets of 15 reps.
- Chins: *Warm up first* with 2 sets of light pulldowns. If you don't have a pull down machine, use a band to warm up by choking it around the top of a squat rack and doing pull downs on your knees. Perform 5 sets with body weight for no more than 10 reps. 2 sets of as many as 10 reps, pronated. 3 sets of as many as 10 reps, supinated. Stagger the sets. No neutral grip on these for this template. If you get shoulder pain when pronated, do all sets supinated. If you can not do any chins unassisted, choke a band around the chin up bar and put it under your feet. Use the weakest band possible. As soon as you can perform two or more chins, begin to do them for as many sets as you can, maximum 5 sets.
- Hammer Curls: 2 sets of 12-15 reps.

The Templates

Deadlift- Technique/Speed Template, Assistance Variant #3

(5x8- wide grip bench, barbell rows, chins, low rep floor press)

Bench (1):

- Flat Bench Press (Competition Grip): 80% 1RM (77.5% first mesocycle), 4 sets of 2 repetitions, followed by 5th set of AMRAP.

  ***Add 5 pounds to the bar per cycle for 5 microcycles or until you are only able to perform 3 reps on the 5thSet, which ever comes FIRST. At this point deload all training for one microcycle. Start over with 80% and go for rep PRs on 5thSets whenever possible.

- Floor Press (1/2 of a thumb from the smooth): 3 sets of 5 reps, first set use 60% of 1RM. Add 5 lbs the following cycle every time you get your target reps for all sets.

- Side Raises: 2 progressive sets of 10 reps, start sub-max and move up each week until you are near a 10RM, then maintain the weight as this will become static volume for now. Try to slow down the negative portion of each rep.

- Rear Raises: Same directions and volume as Side Raises, except you will shoot for 12 reps and focus on maintaining tension, not allowing the dumbbells to come all of the way down.

Squat (2):

- Squat: 80% 1RM for 4 sets of 2 reps followed by 5th set of AMRAP. Move up 5 per cycle, same rules as bench.
- Reverse Hyper: 5 sets of 8 reps.
- Barbell Rows (overhand): 5 sets of 8 reps, start with a medium weight and add 5 pounds to the bar the following cycle and whenever target reps are reached for all 5 sets.
- Heavy Barbell Shrugs: 5 sets of 8, same rules.
- Calf Raises: 5 sets of 8 reps.

Bench (3):

- Wide Grip Bench (2 fingers wider than comp): 5 sets of 8 reps. Start with a medium weight, moving the bar in a focused and controlled manner. Add 5 pounds the following microcycle whenever target reps are reached for all 5 sets.
- Rolling Tricep Ext: 2 progressive sets of 12-20 reps. First set should be very easy. The first cycle do 12 reps, the next cycle 15 reps, next 18, next 20, next: +5lbs x 12 reps, repeat.
- Cable Tricep Ext: 2 sets of 25 reps each arm, overhand; followed by 2 sets of 25 reps each arm, underhand. Use the same weight on all 4 set, if you get 25 reps on all sets for 2 cycles, move up 5 pounds.
- Band Pull Aparts: 3 sets of 30-35 reps, 60 seconds rest between sets. Move down to 45 seconds rest after 2 weeks, then up the reps to 35 with 60 seconds, then 35 reps with 45 seconds, then add a 4th set and follow that pattern. Do not go above 5 sets.

Deadlift (4):

- Deadlift (Competition): 70% 1RM, 5 sets of 3 repetitions, add 5 pounds per microcycle. The emphasis is going to be on technique and speed off the floor.
- Rack Pulls(below knee): 70% 1RM, 3 sets of 3 reps.
- Rev Hyper or Pull Throughs: 3 sets of 15 reps.
- Chins: Warm up first with 2 sets of light pulldowns. If you don't have a pull down machine, use a band to warm up by choking it around the top of a squat rack and doing pull downs on your knees. Start with body weight. Perform 5 sets of 8 reps. Stagger your grip from set to set. (Pronated, neutral, supinated.) You can vary the grip however you like, but however you choose, keep that pattern for at least one mesocycle. When you reach target reps on all sets add a chain the following microcycle or use a belt to load weight.

The Templates

Deadlift- Technique/Speed Template, Assistance Variant #4

(5x8- incline dumbbell bench, dumbbell rows, chins, low rep board press)

Bench (1):

- Flat Bench Press (Competition Grip): 80% 1RM (77.5% first mesocycle), 4 sets of 2 repetitions, followed by 5th set of AMRAP.

  ***Add 5 pounds to the bar per cycle for 5 microcycles or until you are only able to perform 3 reps on the 5thSet, which ever comes FIRST. At this point deload all training for one microcycle. Start over with 80% and go for rep PRs on 5thSets whenever possible.

- 2 board press (1/2 of a thumb from the smooth): 3 sets of 5 reps, first cycle use 60% of full ROM 1RM, second cycle and whenever target reps are reached for all sets add 5 pounds.

- Side Raises: 2 progressive sets of 10 reps, start sub-max and move up each week until you are near a 10RM, then maintain the weight as this will become static volume for now. Try to slow down the negative portion of each rep.

- Rear Raises: Same directions and volume as Side Raises, except you will shoot for 12 reps and focus on maintaining tension, not allowing the dumbbells to come all of the way down.

Squat (2):

- Squat: 80% 1RM for 4 sets of 2 reps followed by 5th set of AMRAP. Move up 5 per cycle, same rules as bench.
- Reverse Hyper: 5 sets of 10 reps.
- Dumbbell Rows, chest supported on incline bench (both hands): 5 sets of 8 reps, start with a medium intensity weight. Add 5 pounds the following microcycle whenever target reps are reached for all sets.
- Dumbbell Shrugs, chest supported on incline bench: 3 sets of 20 reps, same rules.
- Calf Raises: 5 sets of 8 reps.

Bench (3):

- Incline Dumbbell Press (45 degree bench, neutral grip): Start with a medium weight for 5 sets of 8 reps. Perform this movement in a focused, controlled manner. When you get the target reps on all sets, move up 5 lbs the following week.
- Rolling Tricep Ext: 2 progressive sets of 12-20 reps. First set should be very easy. The first cycle do 12 reps, the next cycle 15 reps, next 18, next 20, next: +5lbs x 12 reps, repeat.
- Cable Tricep Ext: 2 sets of 25 reps each arm, overhand; followed by 2 sets of 25 reps each arm, underhand. Use the same weight on all 4 set, if you get 25 reps on all sets for 2 weeks, move up 5 pounds.
- Band Pull Aparts: 3 sets of 30-35 reps, 60 seconds rest between sets. Move down to 45 seconds rest after 2 weeks, then up the reps to 35 with 60 seconds, then 35 reps with 45 seconds, then add a 4th set and follow that pattern. Do not go above 5 sets.

Deadlift (4):

- Deadlift (Competition): 70% 1RM, 5 sets of 3 repetitions, add 5 pounds per microcycle. The emphasis is going to be on technique and speed off the floor.
- Rack Pulls(below knee): 70% 1RM, 3 sets of 3 reps.
- Rev Hyper or Pull Throughs: 3 sets of 15 reps.
- Chins: *Warm up first* with 2 sets of light pulldowns. If you don't have a pull down machine, use a band to warm up by choking it around the top of a squat rack and doing pull downs on your knees. Start with body weight. Stagger your grip from set to set. (Pronated, neutral, supinated.) You can vary the grip however you like, but however you do choose, keep that pattern for at least one mesocycle. When you reach target reps on all sets add a chain the following microcycle or use a belt to load weight.

Squat- Technique/speed Template, Assistance Variant #1

(wide grip rep bench, floor press, barbell rows, high rep chins)

Bench (1):

- Flat Bench Press (Competition Grip): 80% 1RM (77.5% first mesocycle), 4 sets of 2 repetitions, followed by 5th set of AMRAP.

  ***Add 5 pounds to the bar per cycle for 5 microcycles or until you are only able to perform 3 reps on the 5thSet, which ever comes FIRST. At this point deload all training for one microcycle. Start over with 80% and go for rep PRs on 5thSets whenever possible.

- Floor Press (1/2 of a thumb from the smooth): 2 sets of 15 reps, first set use 45% 1RM, second set start with same weight. Hold the first set and add 5 lbs to the second set the following cycle, every time you get all of your target reps.

- Side Raises: 2 progressive sets of 10 reps, start sub-max and move up each cycle until you are near a 10RM, then maintain the weight as this will become static volume for now. Try to slow down the negative portion of each rep.

- Rear Raises: Same directions and volume as Side Raises, except you will shoot for 12 reps and focus on maintaining tension, not allowing the dumbbells to come all of the way down.

Squat (2):

- Squat: 70% 1RM, 5 sets of 3 reps, add 5 pounds per microcycle. The emphasis is going to be on technique and speed.

- Front Squat: 70% 1RM, 3 sets of 3 reps. On your first microcycle, take a rep max and use the coefficient table (Estimating 1RM's section) to determine 1RM. Start with 70% the following cycle and add 5 pounds per cycle.

- Reverse Hyper: 5 sets of 10 reps.

- Barbell Rows (overhand): 2 progressive sets of 12 reps. Start with medium weight and add to the second set the following cycle whenever target(12) reps are achieved.

- Heavy dumbbell rows to lower chest: 1 set of 15 reps, move up next week whenever target reps are achieved.

- Heavy Barbell Shrugs: 2 progressive sets of 15, same rules.

- Calf Raises: 5 sets of 10 reps.

Bench (3):

- Wide Grip Bench (2 fingers wider than comp): 52.5% for 2 sets of 25 reps. When you get 25 on both sets, move up 5 lbs the following week.

- Rolling Tricep Ext: 2 progressive sets of 12-20 reps. First set should be very easy. The first cycle do 12 reps, the next cycle 15 reps, next 18, next 20, next: +5lbs x 12 reps, repeat.

- Cable Tricep Ext: 2 sets of 25 reps each arm, overhand; followed by 2 sets of 25 reps each arm, underhand. Use the same weight on all 4 set. When you get 25 reps on all sets for 2 cycles, move up 5 pounds.

- Band Pull Aparts: 3 sets of 30-35 reps, 60 seconds rest between sets. Move down to 45 seconds rest after 2 cycles, then up the reps to 35 with 60 seconds, then 35 reps with 45 seconds, then add a 4th set and follow that pattern. Do not go above 5 sets.

Deadlift (4):

- Deadlift (Competition): 80% 1RM for 4 sets of 2 reps followed by 5th set of AMRAP. Move up 5 per week, same rules as bench.
- Rev Hyper or Pull Throughs: 3 sets of 15 reps.
- Chins: *Warm up first* with 2 sets of light pulldowns. If you don't have a pull down machine, use a band to warm up by choking it around the top of a squat rack and doing pull downs on your knees. Start with body weight- 1 set for max reps, pronated. 1 set for max reps, supinated. When you can get 20 reps on both sets add a chain the following microcycle or use a belt to load weight. (If you cant do at least 5 chins, pick the template with chins for high sets.) No neutral grip on these for this template. If you get shoulder pain when pronated (overhand), do both sets supinated.
- Hammer Curls: 2 progressive sets of 12-15 reps.

The Templates

Squat- Technique/Speed Template, Assistance Variant #2

(incline dumbbell rep bench, board press, dumbbell rows, high set chins)

Bench (1):

- Flat Bench Press (Competition Grip): 80% 1RM (77.5% first mesocycle), 4 sets of 2 repetitions, followed by 5th set of AMRAP.

  ***Add 5 pounds to the bar per cycle for 5 microcycles or until you are only able to perform 3 reps on the 5thSet, which ever comes FIRST. At this point deload all training for one microcycle. Start over with 80% and go for rep PRs on 5thSets whenever possible.

- 2 board press (1/2 of a thumb from the smooth): 2 sets of 15 reps, first set use 45% of full ROM 1RM, second set start with same weight. Hold the first set and add 5 lbs to the second set the following cycle, every time you get all of your target reps.

- Side Raises: 2 progressive sets of 10 reps, start sub-max and move up each cycle until you are near a 10RM, then maintain the weight as this will become static volume for now. Try to slow down the negative portion of each rep.

- Rear Raises: Same directions and volume as Side Raises, except you will shoot for 12 reps and focus on maintaining tension, not allowing the dumbbells to come all of the way down.

Squat (2):

- Squat: 70% 1RM, 5 sets of 3 reps, add 5 pounds per microcycle. The emphasis is going to be on technique and speed.

- Front Squat: 70% 1RM, 3 sets of 3 reps. On your first microcycle, take a rep max and use the coefficient table (Estimating 1RM's section) to determine 1RM. Start with 70% the following cycle and add 5 pounds per cycle.

- Reverse Hyper: 5 sets of 10 reps.

- Dumbbell Rows, chest supported on incline bench (both hands): 3 sets of 20 reps, start with a medium intensity weight and add to the second set the following cycle whenever target (20) reps are achieved.

- Dumbbell Shrugs, chest supported on incline bench: 3 sets of 20 reps, same rules.

- Calf Raises: 5 sets of 10 reps.

Bench (3):

- Incline Dumbbell Press (45 degree bench, neutral grip): medium weight for 30 reps. When you get 30 on both sets, move up 5 lbs the following week.

- Rolling Tricep Ext: 2 progressive sets of 12-20 reps. First set should be very easy. The first cycle do 12 reps, the next cycle 15 reps, next 18, next 20, next: +5lbs x 12 reps, repeat.

- Cable Tricep Ext: 2 sets of 25 reps each arm, overhand; followed by 2 sets of 25 reps each arm, underhand. Use the same weight on all 4 set, if you get 25 reps on all sets for 2 cycles, move up 5 pounds.

- Band Pull Aparts: 3 sets of 30-35 reps, 60 seconds rest between sets. Move down to 45 seconds rest after 2 cycles, then up the reps to 35 with 60 seconds, then 35 reps with 45 seconds, then add a 4th set and follow that pattern. Do not go above 5 sets.

Deadlift (4):

- Deadlift (Competition): 80% 1RM for 4 sets of 2 reps followed by 5th set of AMRAP. Move up 5 per week, same rules as bench.

- Rev Hyper or Pull Throughs: 3 sets of 15 reps.

- Chins: *Warm up first* with 2 sets of light pulldowns. If you don't have a pull down machine, use a band to warm up by choking it around the top of a squat rack and doing pull downs on your knees. Perform 5 sets with body weight for no more than 10 reps. 2 sets of as many as 10 reps, pronated. 3 sets of as many as 10 reps, supinated. Stagger the sets. No neutral grip on these for this template. If you get shoulder pain when pronated (overhand), do all sets supinated. If you can not do any chins unassisted, choke a band around the chin up bar and put it under your feet. Use the weakest band possible. As soon as you can perform two or more chins, begin to do them for as many sets as you can, maximum 5 sets.

- Hammer Curls: 2 sets of 12-15 reps.

Squat- Technique/Speed Template, Assistance Variant #3

(5x8- wide grip bench, barbell rows, chins, low rep floor press)

Bench (1):

- Flat Bench Press (Competition Grip): 80% 1RM (77.5% first mesocycle), 4 sets of 2 repetitions, followed by 5th set of AMRAP.

    ***Add 5 pounds to the bar per cycle for 5 microcycles or until you are only able to perform 3 reps on the 5thSet, which ever comes FIRST. At this point deload all training for one microcycle. Start over with 80% and go for rep PRs on 5thSets whenever possible.

- Floor Press (1/2 of a thumb from the smooth): 3 sets of 5 reps, first set use 60% of 1RM. Add 5 lbs the following cycle every time you get your target reps for all sets.

- Side Raises: 2 progressive sets of 10 reps, start sub-max and move up each cycle until you are near a 10RM, then maintain the weight as this will become static volume for now. Try to slow down the negative portion of each rep.

- Rear Raises: Same directions and volume as Side Raises, except you will shoot for 12 reps and focus on maintaining tension, not allowing the dumbbells to come all of the way down.

Squat (2):

- Squat: 70% 1RM, 5 sets of 3 reps, add 5 pounds per microcycle. The emphasis is going to be on technique and speed.

- Front Squat: 70% 1RM, 3 sets of 3 reps. On your first microcycle, take a rep max and use the coefficient table (Estimating 1RM's section) to determine 1RM. Start with 70% the following cycle and add 5 pounds per cycle.

- Reverse Hyper: 5 sets of 8 reps.

- Barbell Rows (overhand): 5 sets of 8 reps, start with a medium weight and add 5 pounds to the bar the following cycle and whenever target reps are reached for all 5 sets.

- Heavy Barbell Shrugs: 5 sets of 8, same rules.

- Calf Raises: 5 sets of 8 reps.

Bench (3):

- Wide Grip Bench (2 fingers wider than comp): 5 sets of 8 reps. Start with a medium heavy weight, moving the bar in a focused and controlled manner. Add 5 pounds the following cycle whenever target reps are reached for all 5 sets.

- Rolling Tricep Ext: 2 progressive sets of 12-20 reps. First set should be very easy. The first cycle do 12 reps, the next cycle 15 reps, next 18, next 20, next: +5lbs x 12 reps, repeat.

- Cable Tricep Ext: 2 sets of 25 reps each arm, overhand; followed by 2 sets of 25 reps each arm, underhand. Use the same weight on all 4 set, if you get 25 reps on all sets for 2 cycles, move up 5 pounds.

The Templates

- Band Pull Aparts: 3 sets of 30-35 reps, 60 seconds rest between sets. Move down to 45 seconds rest after 2 cycles, then up the reps to 35 with 60 seconds, then 35 reps with 45 seconds, then add a 4th set and follow that pattern. Do not go above 5 sets.

Deadlift (4):

- Deadlift (Competition): 80% 1RM for 4 sets of 2 reps followed by 5th set of AMRAP. Move up 5 per week, same rules as bench.
- Reverse Hyper or Pull Throughs: 3 sets of 15 reps.
- Chins: *Warm up first* with 2 sets of light pulldowns. If you don't have a pull down machine, use a band to warm up by choking it around the top of a squat rack and doing pull downs on your knees. Start with body weight for 5 sets of 8 reps. Stagger your grip from set to set. (Pronated, neutral, supinated.) You can vary the grip however you like, but however you do choose, keep that pattern for at least one mesocycle. When you reach target reps on all sets add a chain the following microcycle or use a belt to load weight.

The Templates

Squat- Technique/Speed Template, Assistance Variant #4

(5x8- incline dumbbell bench, dumbbell rows, chins, low rep board press)

Bench (1):

- Flat Bench Press (Competition Grip): 80% 1RM (77.5% first mesocycle), 4 sets of 2 repetitions, followed by 5th set of AMRAP.

  ***Add 5 pounds to the bar per cycle for 5 microcycles or until you are only able to perform 3 reps on the 5thSet, which ever comes FIRST. At this point deload all training for one microcycle. Start over with 80% and go for rep PRs on 5thSets whenever possible.

- 2 board press (1/2 of a thumb from the smooth): 3 sets of 5 reps, first cycle use 60% of full ROM 1RM. The second cycle, and whenever target reps are reached for all sets, add 5 pounds.

- Side Raises: 2 progressive sets of 10 reps, start sub-max and move up each cycle until you are near a 10RM, then maintain the weight as this will become static volume for now. Try to slow down the negative portion of each rep.

- Rear Raises: Same directions and volume as Side Raises, except you will shoot for 12 reps and focus on maintaining tension, not allowing the dumbbells to come all of the way down.

Squat (2):

- Squat: 70% 1RM, 5 sets of 3 reps, add 5 pounds per microcycle. The emphasis is going to be on technique and speed.

- Front Squat: 70% 1RM, 3 sets of 3 reps. On your first microcycle, take a rep max and use the coefficient table (Estimating 1RM's section) to determine 1RM. Start with 70% the following cycle and add 5 pounds per cycle.

- Reverse Hyper: 5 sets of 10 reps.

- Dumbbell Rows, chest supported on incline bench (both hands): 5 sets of 8 reps, start with a medium intensity weight. Add 5 pounds the following microcycle whenever target reps are reached for all sets.

- Dumbbell Shrugs, chest supported on incline bench: 3 sets of 20 reps, same rules.

- Calf Raises: 5 sets of 8 reps.

Bench (3):

- Incline Dumbbell Press (45 degree bench, neutral grip): Start with a medium weight for 5 sets of 8 reps. Perform this movement in a focused, controlled manner. When you get the target reps on all sets, move up 5 lbs the following cycle.

- Rolling Tricep Ext: 2 progressive sets of 12-20 reps. First set should be very easy. The first cycle do 12 reps, the next cycle 15 reps, next 18, next 20, next: +5lbs x 12 reps, repeat.

- Cable Tricep Ext: 2 sets of 25 reps each arm, overhand; followed by 2 sets of 25 reps each arm, underhand. Use the same weight on all 4 set, if you get 25 reps on all sets for 2 weeks, move up 5 pounds.

- Band Pull Aparts: 3 sets of 30-35 reps, 60 seconds rest between sets. Move down to 45 seconds rest after 2 cycles, then up the reps to 35 with 60 seconds, then 35 reps with 45 seconds, then add a 4th set and follow that pattern. Do not go above 5 sets.

Deadlift (4):

- Deadlift (Competition): 80% 1RM for 4 sets of 2 reps followed by 5th set of AMRAP. Move up 5 per week, same rules as bench.
- Rev Hyper or Pull Throughs: 3 sets of 15 reps.
- Chins: *Warm up first* with 2 sets of light pulldowns. If you don't have a pull down machine, use a band to warm up by choking it around the top of a squat rack and doing pull downs on your knees. Start with body weight for 5 sets of 8 reps. Stagger your grip from set to set. (Pronated, neutral, supinated.) You can vary the grip however you like, but however you do choose, keep that pattern for at least one mesocycle. When you reach target reps on all sets add a chain the following microcycle or use a belt to load weight.

Low Recoverability- Deadlift- Technique/Speed Template

(wide grip rep bench, floor press, barbell rows, high rep chins)

Bench (1):

- Flat Bench Press (Competition Grip): 72.5% 1RM, 4 sets of 2 repetitions, followed by 5th set of AMRAP.

    ***Add 5 pounds to the bar per cycle for 5 microcycles or until you are only able to perform 3 reps on the 5thSet, which ever comes FIRST. At this point deload all training for one microcycle. Start over with 80% and go for rep PRs on 5thSets whenever possible.

- 2 Board Press (1/2 of a thumb from the smooth): 2 sets of 15 reps, first set use 45% of full ROM 1RM, second set start with same weight. Hold the first set and add 5 lbs to the second set the following week, every time you get all of your target reps.

- Side Raises: 1 set of 10 reps, start sub-max and move up each cycle until you are near a 10RM, then maintain the weight as this will become static volume. Try to slow down the negative portion of each rep.

- Rear Raises: Same directions and volume as Side Raises, except you will shoot for 12 reps and focus on maintaining tension, not allowing the dumbbells to come all of the way down.

Squat (2):

- Squat: 72.5% 1RM for 4 sets of 2 reps followed by 5th set of AMRAP. Move up 5 pounds per cycle, same rules as bench.

- Reverse Hyper: 3 sets of 10 reps.

- Barbell Rows (overhand): 2 progressive sets of 12 reps, start with medium weight and add to the second set the following cycle whenever target(12) reps are achieved.
- Heavy Barbell Shrugs: 2 progressive sets of 15, same rules.
- Calf Raises: 3 sets of 10 reps.

Bench (3):

- Wide Grip Bench (2 fingers wider than comp): 52.5% for 1 set of 25 reps. When you get 25 reps, move up 5 lbs the following cycle.
- Rolling Tricep Ext: 2 progressive sets of 12-20 reps. First set should be very easy. The first cycle do 12 reps, the next cycle 15 reps, next 18, next 20, next: +5lbs x 12 reps, repeat.
- Cable Tricep Ext: 2 sets of 25 reps each arm, overhand or underhand. Use the same weight on all both sets, if you get 25 reps on both sets for 2 cycles, move up 5 pounds.
- Band Pull Aparts: 3 sets of 30-35 reps, 60 seconds rest between sets. Move down to 45 seconds rest after 2 cycles, then up the reps to 35 with 60 seconds, then 35 reps with 45 seconds, then add a 4th set and follow that pattern. Do not go above 5 sets.

Deadlift (4):

- Deadlift (Competition): 70% 1RM, 5 sets of 3 repetitions, add 5 pounds per microcycle. The emphasis is going to be on technique and speed off the floor.
- Rack Pulls(below knee): 70% 1RM, 2 sets of 3 reps.
- Reverse Hyper or Pull Throughs: 2 sets of 15 reps.

- Chins: *Warm up first* with 2 sets of light pulldowns. If you don't have a pull down machine, use a band to warm up by choking it around the top of a squat rack and doing pull downs on your knees. Start with body weight- 1 set for max reps, pronated. 1 set for max reps, supinated. When you can get 20 reps on both sets, add a chain the following microcycle or use a belt to load weight. (If you cant do at least 5 chins, pick the template with chins for high sets.) No neutral grip on these for this template. If you get shoulder pain when pronated (overhand), do both sets supinated.

The Templates

Low Recoverability- Squat- Technique/Speed Template

(wide grip rep bench, floor press, barbell rows, high rep chins)

Bench (1):

- Flat Bench Press (Competition Grip): 72.5% 1RM, 4 sets of 2 repetitions, followed by 5th set of AMRAP.
  ***Add 5 pounds to the bar per cycle for 5 microcycles or until you are only able to perform 3 reps on the 5thSet, which ever comes FIRST. At this point deload all training for one microcycle. Start over with 80% and go for rep PRs on 5thSets whenever possible.

- 2 Board Press (1/2 of a thumb from the smooth): 2 sets of 15 reps, first set use 45% of full ROM 1RM, second set start with same weight. Hold the first set and add 5 lbs to the second set the following cycle, every time you get all of your target reps.

- Side Raises: 1 set of 10 reps, start sub-max and move up each cycle until you are near a 10RM, then maintain the weight as this will become static volume. Try to slow down the negative portion of each rep.

- Rear Raises: Same directions as Side Raises, except you will shoot for 12 reps and focus on maintaining tension, not allowing the dumbbells to come all of the way down.

Squat (2):

- Squat: 70% 1RM, 5 sets of 3 repetitions, add 5 pounds per microcycle. The emphasis is going to be on technique and speed.

- Front Squat: 70% 1RM, 2 sets of 3 reps. On your first microcycle, take a rep max and use the coefficient table (Estimating 1RM's section) to determine 1RM. Start with 70% the following cycle and add 5 pounds per cycle.

- Reverse Hyper: 3 sets of 10 reps.

- Barbell Rows (overhand): 2 progressive sets of 12 reps, start with medium weight and add to the second set the following cycle whenever target reps are achieved.

- Heavy Barbell Shrugs: 2 progressive sets of 15, same rules.

- Calf Raises: 3 sets of 10 reps.

Bench (3):

- Wide Grip Bench (2 fingers wider than comp): 52.5% for 1 set of 25 reps. When you get 25 reps, move up 5 lbs the following cycle.

- Rolling Tricep Ext: 2 progressive sets of 12-20 reps. First set should be very easy. The first cycle do 12 reps, the next cycle 15 reps, next 18, next 20, next: +5lbs x 12 reps, repeat.

- Cable Tricep Ext: 2 sets of 25 reps each arm, overhand or underhand. Use the same weight on all both sets, if you get 25 reps on both sets for 2 cycles, move up 5 pounds.

- Band Pull Aparts: 3 sets of 30-35 reps, 60 seconds rest between sets. Move down to 45 seconds rest after 2 weeks, then up the reps to 35 with 60 seconds, then 35 reps with 45 seconds, then add a 4th set and follow that pattern. Do not go above 5 sets.

Deadlift (4):

- Deadlift (Competition): 72.5% 1RM for 4 sets of 2 reps followed by 5th set of AMRAP. Move up 5 per week, same rules as bench.
- Rev Hyper or Pull Throughs: 2 sets of 15 reps.
- Chins: *Warm up first* with 2 sets of light pulldowns. If you don't have a pull down machine, use a band to warm up by choking it around the top of a squat rack and doing pull downs on your knees. Start with body weight- 1 set for max reps, pronated. 1 set for max reps, supinated. When you can get 20 reps on both sets add a chain the following microcycle or use a belt to load weight. (If you cant do at least 5 chins, pick the template with chins for high sets.) No neutral grip on these for this template. If you get shoulder pain when pronated (overhand), do both sets supinated.

Low Recoverability- Deadlift- Technique/Speed Template

(75% Bench/Squat wide grip rep bench, floor press, barbell rows, high rep chins)

Bench (1):

- Flat Bench Press (Competition Grip): 75% 1RM, 4 sets of 2 repetitions, followed by 5th set of AMRAP.

    ***Add 5 pounds to the bar per cycle for 5 microcycles or until you are only able to perform 3 reps on the 5thSet, which ever comes FIRST. At this point deload all training for one microcycle. Start over with 80% and go for rep PRs on 5thSets whenever possible.

- 2 Board Press (1/2 of a thumb from the smooth): 2 sets of 15 reps, first set use 45% of full ROM 1RM, second set start with same weight. Hold the first set and add 5 lbs to the second set the following cycle, every time you get all of your target reps.

- Side Raises: 1 set of 10 reps, start sub-max and move up each cycle until you are near a 10RM, then maintain the weight as this will become static volume. Try to slow down the negative portion of each rep.

- Rear Raises: Same directions as Side Raises, except you will shoot for 12 reps and focus on maintaining tension, not allowing the dumbbells to come all of the way down.

Squat (2):

- Squat: 75% 1RM, 4 sets of 2 repetitions, followed by 5th set of AMRAP. Same rules as bench.
- Reverse Hyper: 3 sets of 10 reps.
- Barbell Rows (overhand): 2 progressive sets of 12 reps, start with medium weight and add to the second set the following cycle whenever target reps are achieved.
- Heavy Barbell Shrugs: 2 progressive sets of 15, same rules.
- Calf Raises: 3 sets of 10 reps.

Bench (3):

- Wide Grip Bench (2 fingers wider than comp): 52.5% for 1 set of 25 reps. When you get 25 reps, move up 5 lbs the following cycle.
- Rolling Tricep Ext: 2 progressive sets of 12-20 reps. First set should be very easy. The first cycle do 12 reps, the next cycle 15 reps, next 18, next 20, next: +5lbs x 12 reps, repeat.
- Cable Tricep Ext: 2 sets of 25 reps each arm, overhand or underhand. Use the same weight on all both sets, if you get 25 reps on both sets for 2 cycles, move up 5 pounds.
- Band Pull Aparts: 3 sets of 30-35 reps, 60 seconds rest between sets. Move down to 45 seconds rest after 2 weeks, then up the reps to 35 with 60 seconds, then 35 reps with 45 seconds, then add a 4th set and follow that pattern. Do not go above 5 sets.

Deadlift (4):

- Deadlift (Competition): 70% 1RM, 5 sets of 3 repetitions, add 5 pounds per microcycle. The emphasis is going to be on technique and speed off the floor.
- Rev Hyper or Pull Throughs: 2 sets of 15 reps.
- Chins: *Warm up first* with 2 sets of light pulldowns. If you don't have a pull down machine, use a band to warm up by choking it around the top of a squat rack and doing pull downs on your knees. Start with body weight- 1 set for max reps, pronated. 1 set for max reps, supinated. When you can get 20 reps on both sets add a chain the following microcycle or use a belt to load weight. (If you cant do at least 5 chins, pick the template with chins for high sets.) No neutral grip on these for this template. If you get shoulder pain when pronated (overhand), do both sets supinated.

The Templates

Low Recoverability- Squat- Technique/Speed Template

(75% Bench/Deadlift wide grip rep bench, floor press, barbell rows, high rep chins)

Bench (1):

- Flat Bench Press (Competition Grip): 75% 1RM, 4 sets of 2 repetitions, followed by 5th set of AMRAP.

  ***Add 5 pounds to the bar per cycle for 5 microcycles or until you are only able to perform 3 reps on the 5thSet, which ever comes FIRST. At this point deload all training for one microcycle. Start over with 80% and go for rep PRs on 5thSets whenever possible.

- 2 Board Press (1/2 of a thumb from the smooth): 2 sets of 15 reps, first set use 45% of full ROM 1RM, second set start with same weight. Hold the first set and add 5 lbs to the second set the following cycle, every time you get all of your target reps.

- Side Raises: 1 set of 10 reps, start sub-max and move up each cycle until you are near a 10RM, then maintain the weight as this will become static volume. Try to slow down the negative portion of each rep.

- Rear Raises: Same directions as Side Raises, except you will shoot for 12 reps and focus on maintaining tension, not allowing the dumbbells to come all of the way down.

Squat (2):

- Squat: 70% 1RM, 5 sets of 3 repetitions, add 5 pounds per microcycle. The emphasis is going to be on technique and speed.

- Reverse hyper: 3 sets of 10 reps.

- Barbell Rows (overhand): 2 progressive sets of 12 reps, start with medium weight and add to the second set the following cycle whenever target reps are achieved.

- Heavy Barbell Shrugs: 2 progressive sets of 15, same rules.

- Calf Raises: 3 sets of 10 reps.

Bench (3):

- Wide Grip Bench (2 fingers wider than comp): 52.5% for 1 set of 25 reps. When you get 25 reps, move up 5 lbs the following cycle.

- Rolling Tricep Ext: 2 progressive sets of 12-20 reps. First set should be very easy. The first cycle do 12 reps, the next cycle 15 reps, next 18, next 20, next: +5lbs x 12 reps, repeat.

- Cable Tricep Ext: 2 sets of 25 reps each arm, overhand or underhand. Use the same weight on all both sets, if you get 25 reps on both sets for 2 cycle, move up 5 pounds.

- Band Pull Aparts: 3 sets of 30-35 reps, 60 seconds rest between sets. Move down to 45 seconds rest after 2 cycle, then up the reps to 35 with 60 seconds, then 35 reps with 45 seconds, then add a 4th set and follow that pattern. Do not go above 5 sets.

Deadlift (4):

- Deadlift (Competition): 75% 1RM for 4 sets of 2 reps followed by 5th set of AMRAP. Move up 5 per week, same rules as bench.

- Rev Hyper or Pull Throughs: 2 sets of 15 reps.

- Chins: *Warm up first* with 2 sets of light pulldowns. If you don't have a pull down machine, use a band to warm up by choking it around the top of a squat rack and doing pull downs on your knees. Start with body weight- 1 set for max reps, pronated. 1 set for max reps, supinated. When you can get 20 reps on both sets add a chain the following microcycle or use a belt to load weight. (If you cant do at least 5 chins, pick the template with chins for high sets.) No neutral grip on these for this template. If you get shoulder pain when pronated (overhand), do both sets supinated.

The Templates
Bench Only Template

(wide grip rep bench, 1" pause press, barbell rows, high rep chins)

Bench (1):

- Flat Bench Press (Competition Grip): 80% 1RM (77.5% first mesocycle), 4 sets of 2 repetitions, followed by 5th set of AMRAP.

  ***Add 5 pounds to the bar per cycle for 5 microcycles or until you are only able to perform 3 reps on the 5thSet, which ever comes FIRST. At this point deload all training for one microcycle. Start over with 80% and go for rep PRs on 5thSets whenever possible.

- 1" Pause Press (competition grip): 3 sets of 5 reps, 60% of full ROM 1RM. Add 5 lbs the following week, every time you get all of your target reps.

- Side Raises: 2 progressive sets of 10 reps, start sub-max and move up each cycle until you are near a 10RM, then maintain the weight as this will become static volume. Try to slow down the negative portion of each rep.

- Rear Raises: Same directions and volume as Side Raises, except you will shoot for 12 reps and focus on maintaining tension, not allowing the dumbbells to come all of the way down.

Squat (2):

- SSB Squat: 70% 1RM, 3 sets of 5 repetitions, add 5 pounds per microcycle. The emphasis is going to be on focused, controlled movement.

- Reverse hyper: 5 sets of 10 reps.

- Barbell Rows (overhand): 2 progressive sets of 12 reps, start with medium weight and add to the second set the following cycle whenever target reps are achieved.

- Heavy dumbbell rows to lower chest: 1 set of 15 reps, move up next cycle whenever target reps are achieved.

- Heavy Barbell Shrugs: 2 progressive sets of 15, same rules.

- Calf Raises: 5 sets of 10 reps.

Bench (3):

- Wide Grip Bench (2 fingers wider than comp): 52.5% for 2 sets of 25 reps. When you get 25 on both sets, move up 5 lbs the following cycle.

- Rolling Tricep Ext: 2 progressive sets of 12-20 reps. First set should be very easy. The first cycle do 12 reps, the next cycle 15 reps, next 18, next 20, next: +5lbs x 12 reps, repeat.

- Cable Tricep Ext: 2 sets of 25 reps each arm, overhand; followed by 2 sets of 25 reps each arm, underhand. Use the same weight on all 4 set, if you get 25 reps on all sets for 2 cycles, move up 5 pounds.

- Band Pull Aparts: 3 sets of 30-35 reps, 60 seconds rest between sets. Move down to 45 seconds rest after 2 weeks, then up the reps to 35 with 60 seconds, then 35 reps with 45 seconds, then add a 4th set and follow that pattern. Do not go above 5 sets.

Deadlift (4):

- Deadlift (Conventional): 70% 1RM, 3 sets of 5 repetitions, add 5 pounds per microcycle. The emphasis is going to be on focused, controlled reps.

- Rack Pulls (below knee): 60% 1RM, 3 sets of 5 reps.

- Rev Hyper or Pull Throughs: 3 sets of 15 reps.
- Chins: *Warm up first* with 2 sets of light pulldowns. If you don't have a pull down machine, use a band to warm up by choking it around the top of a squat rack and doing pull downs on your knees. Start with body weight- 1 set for max reps, pronated. 1 set for max reps, supinated. When you can get 20 reps on both sets add a chain the following microcycle or use a belt to load weight. No neutral grip on these for this template. If you get shoulder pain when pronated (overhand), do both sets supinated.
- Hammer Curls: 2 progressive sets of 12-15 reps.

The Templates

Garage/Basement Template- Deadlift- Technique/Speed

(wide grip rep bench, floor press, barbell rows, high rep chins)

Bench (1):

- Flat Bench Press (Competition Grip): 80% 1RM (77.5% first mesocycle), 4 sets of 2 repetitions, followed by 5th set of AMRAP.

  ***Add 5 pounds to the bar per cycle for 5 microcycles or until you are only able to perform 3 reps on the 5thSet, which ever comes FIRST. At this point deload all training for one microcycle. Start over with 80% and go for rep PRs on 5thSets whenever possible.

- Floor Press (1/2 of a thumb from the smooth): 2 sets of 15 reps, first set use 45% 1RM, second set start with same weight. Hold the first set and add 5 lbs to the second set the following cycle, every time you get all of your target reps.

- Standing or Seated Over Head Press: 2 progressive sets of 12-20 reps. First set should be very easy. The first cycle do 12 reps, the next cycle 15 reps, next 18, next 20, next: +5lbs x 12 reps, repeat.

Squat (2):

- Squat: 80% 1RM for 4 sets of 2 reps followed by 5th set of AMRAP. Move up 5 per week, same rules as bench.

- Band Pull Through: 5 sets of 10 reps.

- Barbell Rows (overhand): 2 progressive sets of 12 reps, start with medium weight and add to the second set the following cycle whenever target reps are achieved.

- Heavy Barbell Shrugs: 2 progressive sets of 15, same rules.
- Barbell Calf Raises: 5 sets of 10 reps.

Bench (3):

- Wide Grip Bench (2 fingers wider than comp): 52.5% for 2 sets of 25 reps. When you get 25 on both sets, move up 5 lbs the following cycle.
- Barbell Tricep Ext: 2 progressive sets of 12-20 reps. First set should be very easy. The first cycle do 12 reps, the next cycle 15 reps, next 18, next 20, next: +5lbs x 12 reps, repeat.
- Band Pull Aparts: 3 sets of 30-35 reps, 60 seconds rest between sets. Move down to 45 seconds rest after 2 cycles, then up the reps to 35 with 60 seconds, then 35 reps with 45 seconds, then add a 4th set and follow that pattern. Do not go above 5 sets.

Deadlift (4):

- Deadlift (Competition): 70% 1RM, 5 sets of 3 repetitions, add 5 pounds per microcycle. The emphasis is going to be on technique and speed off the floor.
- Rack Pulls(below knee): 70% 1RM, 3 sets of 3 reps.
- Band Pull Throughs: 3 sets of 15 reps.
- Chins: *Warm up first* with 2 sets of light pulldowns. If you don't have a pull down machine, use a band to warm up by choking it around the top of a squat rack and doing pull downs on your knees. Start with body weight- 1 set for max reps, pronated. 1 set for max reps, supinated. When you can get 20 reps on both sets add a chain the following microcycle or use a belt to load weight. (If you cant do at least 5 chins, pick the template with chins for

The Templates

high sets.) If you get shoulder pain when pronated (overhand), do both sets supinated or try neutral grip.

The Templates

Garage/Basement Template- Squat-Technique/Speed

(wide grip rep bench, floor press, barbell rows, high rep chins)

Bench (1):

- Flat Bench Press (Competition Grip): 80% 1RM (77.5% first mesocycle), 4 sets of 2 repetitions, followed by 5th set of AMRAP.

  ***Add 5 pounds to the bar per cycle for 5 microcycles or until you are only able to perform 3 reps on the 5thSet, which ever comes FIRST. At this point deload all training for one microcycle. Start over with 80% and go for rep PRs on 5thSets whenever possible.*

- Floor Press (1/2 of a thumb from the smooth): 2 sets of 15 reps, first set use 45% 1RM, second set start with same weight. Hold the first set and add 5 lbs to the second set the following cycle, every time you get all of your target reps.

- Standing or Seated Over Head Press: 2 progressive sets of 12-20 reps. First set should be very easy. The first cycle do 12 reps, the next cycle 15 reps, next 18, next 20, next: +5lbs x 12 reps, repeat.

Squat (2):

- Squat: 70% 1RM, 5 sets of 3 reps, add 5 pounds per microcycle. The emphasis is going to be on technique and speed.

- Front Squat: 70% 1RM, 3 sets of 3 reps. On your first microcycle, take a rep max and use the coefficient table (Estimating 1RM's section) to determine 1RM. Start with 70% the following cycle and add 5 pounds per cycle.

- Band Pull Through: 5 sets of 10 reps.
- Barbell Rows (overhand): 2 progressive sets of 12 reps, start with medium weight and add to the second set the following cycle whenever target reps are achieved.
- Heavy Barbell Shrugs: 2 progressive sets of 15, same rules.
- Barbell Calf Raises: 5 sets of 10 reps.

Bench (3):

- Wide Grip Bench (2 fingers wider than comp): 52.5% for 2 sets of 25 reps. When you get 25 on both sets, move up 5 lbs the following cycle.
- Barbell Tricep Ext: 2 progressive sets of 12-20 reps. First set should be very easy. The first cycle do 12 reps, the next cycle 15 reps, next 18, next 20, next: +5lbs x 12 reps, repeat.
- Band Pull Aparts: 3 sets of 30-35 reps, 60 seconds rest between sets. Move down to 45 seconds rest after 2 cycles, then up the reps to 35 with 60 seconds, then 35 reps with 45 seconds, then add a 4th set and follow that pattern. Do not go above 5 sets.

Deadlift (4):

- Deadlift (Competition): 80% 1RM for 4 sets of 2 reps followed by 5th set of AMRAP. Move up 5 per week, same rules as bench.
- Band Pull Throughs: 3 sets of 15 reps.
- Chins: *Warm up first* with 2 sets of light pulldowns. If you don't have a pull down machine, use a band to warm up by choking it around the top of a squat rack and doing pull downs on your knees. Start with body weight- 1 set for max reps, pronated. 1 set for max reps, supinated.

When you can get 20 reps on both sets add a chain the following microcycle or use a belt to load weight. (If you cant do at least 5 chins, pick the template with chins for high sets.) If you get shoulder pain when pronated (overhand), do both sets supinated or try neutral grip.

Printed in Great Britain
by Amazon